THE BIG PICTURE

A. Whitney Brown

THE BIG PICTURE

An American Commentary

HarperPerennial

A Division of HarperCollins*Publishers*

FIRST EDITION

Designed by Alma Orenstein

Library of Congress Cataloging-in-Publication Data

Brown, A. Whitney, 1952–
    The Big picture: an American commentary / A. Whitney Brown.
    —1st HarperPerennial ed.
        p.   cm.
    ISBN 0-06-096825-7 (paper)
    1. United States—Politics and government—1981–1989—Humor. 2. United States—Politics and government—1989—Humor. 3. World politics—1985–1995—Humor.   I. Title.
E876.B758   1991
973.92'0207—dc20   90-55050

91 92 93 94 95 AC/FG 10 9 8 7 6 5 4 3 2 1

This book is dedicated to
Anna Klein and Tom Fleming,
two teachers who made a difference.

Contents

CONTENTS

Acknowledgments

I WOULD LIKE TO THANK Lorne Michaels for paying my salary while I wrote this book. I am very grateful to Tom Miller and Jim Hornfischer at HarperCollins, Karen Michael, and my good friends George Manos and Jim Stein.

I also humbly acknowledge my fellow writers at "Saturday Night Live," who contributed many of these ideas, some of them willingly. They are: James Sowney, Al Franken, Eddie Gorodetsky, Billy Kimball, Jon Lovitz, Bruce McCullough, Mark McKinney, George Meyer, Bob Odenkirk, Herb Sargent, and Robert Smigel. Special thanks to Joe Forristal.

Thanks also to copyeditor Jeffrey Smith and Terry Belanger, the proofreader.

Author's Note

I 'VE BEEN ACCUSED of being a humorist, and I deny
it. This book should clear my name. At times I
was tempted to resort to wit, but I resisted.

Unfortunately, through no fault of my own, I
was forced to insert several unserious sentences
at various places. I admit these to be intention-
ally amusing. If, through some careless editing
or malicious typesetting, they are not, well,
that's the saving grace of humor; if you fail, at
least you don't have anyone laughing at you.

PART ONE

The Big Picture Throughout History

1

The Big Picture

THE BIG PICTURE, my friends, is what this book is all about. The wide-screen worldview of that mighty billboard of life. On it is painted the vast panorama of history that makes up the unbounded mural of existence, that intricate illustration of the multicolored mosaic of mankind, the all-encompassing postcard snapshot of humanity *in toto*. In short, what the Spanish so eloquently describe as "El Foto Grande."

What is The Big Picture? You could call it a steel-belted radial spare for the Wheel of Karma, for a world that's riding on mega-retreads. It's something to help us keep track of all the things that have happened since the end of history.

History is a very tricky thing. To begin with, you can't get it mixed up with the past. The past actually happened, but history is only what someone wrote down.

If you don't think there is a difference, just witness an event and then read about it the next day in the *New York Post*. History is made by writers—made up, if they have a deadline. Knowing this exposes one of the greatest mysteries of history: The reason history repeats itself is not a cosmic plan, it's plagiarism.

There was a time when a picture was worth a thousand words. Now a picture is worth $52 million and words aren't worth anything (especially the ones people give you when they don't have any actual cash on hand at the moment).

Things didn't start that way. In the beginning was the Word, according to the Bible. The Bible, incidentally, means "The Book." Although with just one Word, it probably wasn't much of a book at the time. There are some people who will say the above statement is sacrilegious (which just goes to show that all the words added since then haven't done much good).

As mankind went along, he got more garrulous. People spoke softly at that time. Coincidentally, they also carried big sticks, just in case an aging relative repeated a pointless story.

Then suddenly oil companies and pharmaceutical manufacturers began hiring spokesmen, and words started gushing from every hole. Verbal inflation set in.

Private citizens took to hiring lawyers whenever they fell down in the supermarket. People got the idea that if anything bad happened to them anywhere, somebody owed them money.

Soon, nobody would take anybody's word for anything, and there was a glut. Since the supply of truth stayed about the same, it had to be stretched in order to go around. I don't remember the exact time, but I think it was "Morning in America."

Truth was harder to find than a fundamentalist in a public library. That's about when *USA Today* came out, but it could have been a coincidence.

In fact, truth was so scarce that Christian groups ran out of things to censor. They got so hard up they joined forces with militant lesbians to ban bare breasts in magazines. These strange bedfellows eventually managed to get *Playboy* and *Penthouse* pulled off certain convenience-store shelves, claiming that bare breasts are degrading to women.

I won't argue the point, but if these groups were sincere, they would also ban the sale of ultramarine turquoise eye shadow. What could be more degrading than to walk around looking like a tropical fish with a hangover?

Ed Meese was attorney general then, and his primary accomplishment was to make people reappraise the brilliant legal reasoning that marked the work of John Mitchell. Meese hired a commission to find a link between violent sex crimes and pornography, which its members did, and kept their jobs, besides. I don't have any statistics on the matter, and I wouldn't know how to interpret them to prove my point if I did, but if some sex-crazed pervert on the prowl wants to stop by the 7-Eleven and purchase some dirty pictures, I say society should let him. Maybe he'll get his rocks off that way, instead of on some teenage runaway who crosses his path.

Not long ago, I picked up a copy of *USA Today* just to take my mind off world events. I turned to the Life section and was greeted by the cheerful headline: "Cancer Patients Living Longer."

It's not often that good news like this crops up in the print media, or in the case of

USA Today, the large-print media, so I read on. The text boiled down to the following facts: First, more people were getting cancer than ever. Second, it killed them at about the same stage of the disease. The only difference was that they were being diagnosed a year earlier, on the average.

So they weren't living longer, they were just learning they were going to die earlier. The headline should have read, "More Bad News Sooner for Cancer Patients."

I then turned to "Statistics That Shape Our Nation." There I learned that one out of ten adult Americans is functionally illiterate. The article was augmented with drawings and stick figures. Somebody had colored in the weather map on the back. I was glad to know that at least some of that 10 percent had found jobs.

Those 25 million or more of our unlettered fellow citizens may not be reading this book, but we can't ignore them. Sooner or later they will appear at the bar stool next to us, asking us what sign we are and insisting that spacemen built the Pyramids. A few may even vote in our elections.

The strength of our culture is diversity. I've seen hieroglyphs on the subway that would stump Champollion, the man who deciphered the Rosetta stone.

So, rather than campaign fruitlessly against the evils of illiteracy, I decided to go to work writing for television. It has been said that television is the literature of our age. This is obviously untrue, because it is far too popular. I seriously doubt that there has ever been a time when the general population spent six to eight hours a day immersed in literature. It would be safer to say that television is the conversation of our age. From it we get our gossip, our news, and our idle chatter. A good part of it, like conversation in any age, is a long buildup to a sales pitch.

The tribes of mankind are merging under the totem of a single symbiotic organism, and the eye at the top of the pole is television. Because of television, I can go to a remote village in New Guinea, days upriver in a dugout canoe, step up to the most apathetic adolescent, and say "Wubwub, wubwub, nyuck, nyuck, nyuck," and he'll poke his fingers in my eye. TV has made the Three Stooges an ingrained part of the universal preteen experience, and shared memories are the building blocks of a homogeneous culture. It turns people into a People. If it is not too good at making people think, it is *very* good at making people think alike.

The question is, can we really put our worldview in the hands of a medium that changes the name of a planet just because it sounds embarrassing? Dan Rather can mumble "Courage" after every broadcast until the camels come home, but he still won't have the balls to say "Dark-colored rings have been discovered around Uranus." To the cowardice of changing the name, we must add the stupidity of changing it to something pronounced "Úrinus."

The networks try to appear socially responsible. Of course, they can't actually be socially responsible or they'd have the ratings of C-SPAN. So, they vent their public-service zeal with things like anti-crack commercials, writing off unsold commercial time on the late-night airwaves, and, more important, taking a courageous stand against the formidable pro-crack lobby.

The networks know exactly who watches which programs. They spend a lot of money on research to find this out, because it enables them to target commercials to the right viewers. You can learn a lot about the life-style of the people who watch a given program by observing the commercials aimed at them. For example, you never see exercise equipment advertised during a football game.

The commercials on the network news have changed a lot since I was a kid. They used to advertise cars, antacids, dog food, and toothpaste. In other words, the average viewer drove a car, worked in a stressful job, had a house with a yard and a social life. He was a mainstream consumer.

Now the commercials are a litany of elderly ills; Porcelana, Polident, Preparation H, gentle laxatives, and insurance you can't be turned down for at any age. The people who watched the network news in the fifties are the only ones still watching it. They must be very well informed by now, which is good, since they are also the only ones who vote. Today's mainstream consumer watches "Wheel of Fortune" and couldn't care less about the events of the world or even who runs the country. What passes for news reflects this. It's entertaining. A girl down a well is video gold, genocide in Uganda is pretty much four-day-old fish.

Television brings the whole world into every home, providing everyone a way to escape from it. It does this in different ways, though. Consider the difference between Soviet and American television. In America, the purpose of television is to sell people consumer junk. In the Soviet Union, its purpose is to explain to people why there's no consumer junk to buy.

The ancient Chinese had a curse: "May you live in interesting times." I suppose they had time to think of wise curses like that because they didn't have CNN.

No question, we live in interesting times. We have a hole in our ozone, acid rain, giant hurricanes, fires, floods, epidemics, and droughts. Species are becoming extinct before we've even had a chance to exploit them.

Signs of the Apocalypse are everywhere. Milli Vanilli won a Grammy for best new artist. Last year the Knicks made the play-offs. They may do it again. We may even live to read about it in the *New York Post*. A giant screaming headline: "KNICKS WIN!!" And then, in tiny little letters on the fourth page, "World Ends."

The fundamental flaw with the press, both print and electronic, is that it deals in current events. We're drowning in a flood of information: wars, coups, scandals, natural disasters, sensational crimes, economic crises, political shenanigans. I could go on and on, but there's no use beating a dead horse.[*] We no longer have history, only news.

[*] I mean, aside from the pure joy of it.

*   *   *

There's a lot we should be able to learn from history. And yet history proves that we never do. In fact, the main lesson of history is that we never learn the lessons of history. This makes us look so stupid that few people care to read it. They'd rather not be reminded. Any good history book is mainly just a long list of mistakes, complete with names and dates. It's very embarrassing.

The end of history is pretty good news for the kids in our schools who have to pretend to learn it. As any business major will tell you, there's no future in it. We've won the war of ideologies, democracy is sweeping the planet, even the Communists are anti-Communist. It took forty-five years, but the cold war is over, and now we can take all that energy and money and talent we've been wasting against the Soviets and turn it against each other. The future is a lot closer than the past ever was.

But in The Big Picture, if you're standing way back, squinting your eyes, and you've got the light of the moon just right, through polarized Ray Bans, you can just see far enough into the past to notice that almost all the things that unite us as Americans are in our history. You can plainly see enough to love us for it, where we came from and what we stand for, and it makes you feel good enough not to sue somebody that day.

You can also see enough to fear what we might turn into. But most of all what I see in The Big Picture makes me hope we can be more than we are.

I love America. I even vacation here. I drink the water, straight from the tap, even in Florida. I can't fathom why Americans buy water from overseas. It's water, *water*! It isn't even supposed to *have* a taste. On the other hand, water from France probably is better because there's a good chance no one has ever bathed in it.

For some people it's easy to love America, but I have to work at it. It keeps changing, for one thing. It never tells me where it's going anymore. Sometimes I just sit there and look at it for hours, watching it sleep. But I worry. What's going to happen when it has to go out and face the real world?

It's easier to love something if you know what it is. Most other countries have some way of defining themselves as a people. The British, for example, have their history, their finest hour, their Royal Relics, and their never-setting sun, and they sit on the porch watching their mighty grandchildren grow. The Germans have the Fatherland, and if they ever need an ego boost, there's France right next door. The French, in turn, have their language. Even the Germans can't spell it. Be they in Quebec, Haiti, or Paris, Frenchmen and Frenchwomen are united by the mother tongue.

The Japanese have their Japaneseness, and even the Canadians, with all their separatist squabbles, share the powerful bond that, one and all, they aren't Americans, eh? You can see them on vacation in Latin America, buttonholing street peddlers and shouting, "I'm *not* an American, I'm a *Canadian*. Me no gringo! Canadian! You know? No CIA! No gringo, me."

But America isn't just a piece of land with leaky borders. Neither do we all share the same language. Far from it. Our neighbors to the south at least all go to the same church.

To make things worse, Americans have a lazy habit of defining themselves in terms of what they are against rather than what they believe in. Why waste time constructing a set of principles when the world is full of evil empires to hate?

While the people of the world find ways to become more like us, we find ways to become less like each other. The shrewishness of single-issue politics is poisoning traditional coalitions. Dogmatism hamstrings ethical debate, and the fear of drugs, disease, and racial tension hounds us.

The nations that come after us to freedom deserve more than a paint-by-number portrait of greed as a role model. It was Andrew Carnegie, founder of U.S. Steel, who said, "A man who dies rich dies disgraced." In the broad brush strokes of The Big Picture, ideas alone are the convertible currency of mankind.

Current events, as we shall see, are nothing more than a teeming school of red herring in the vast sea of history, clogging the nets of those who strain for truth. This book is a tale of a stately ship adrift in that unforgiving sea. I see her caught in dangerous currents while the captain gives speeches about what a pretty pale blue the water is becoming.

We're awash in a sea of information.

This is my signal to our stately ship as she cruises that unforgiving sea. She is running in the shallow straits of self-interest while her helmsman flies full sail with the shifting winds of opinion, steering blind through an oily mist of avarice, guided by bellowing foghorns of oversimplification toward a whirlpool of cynicism and shortsightedness. I have to admit the food is good, though.

Somehow she remains the vessel of hope for common swabbies around the world. They come in their rafts and dugouts, boat people riding the crest of a rising tidal wave of global interdependence. They feel the spray on their faces, not knowing it's blown from the curl of a tsunami bringing in the millennium and sweeping the ancient cultural antagonisms of our species into foam and smashing them onto the rapidly eroding beach of an impending planetary shipwreck.

Somewhere ahead the beacon of national consensus still shines, but the common ground on which it stands seems to forever recede before us, like the horizon.

This is the tale of a hopeful mariner. It's not all true, but you can believe it anyway. The most reliable sailor is one who never learned to swim.

2

Why the Trump Shuttle Will Never Match the Pyramids

"Vanity of vanities, saith the Preacher, all is *vanity."*

—ECCLESIASTES 1:2

EVERYBODY wants to be remembered for something. Custer wanted to be President. Instead he will be remembered as the last high-ranking American military officer to die from a stone-age weapon. Actually, a number of them.

*   *   *

The Big Picture is littered with monuments to Man's vanity. The pyramids of Egypt are the largest and most egregious example of this innate character flaw in the human race. The Great Pyramid exacted an enormous toll of human suffering among the common Egyptians who were forced to build it. They came to despise Cheops as a tyrant, and when he died, they tried to erase his memory by naming the pyramid after a shepherd who grazed his sheep in the neighborhood, Philition. This is all according to Herodotus, a notorious historical liar.

The Taj Mahal in Agra, India, was originally built to impress a Mughal's dead girlfriend, but he liked it so much he made a tomb for himself out of it.

Mount Rushmore is one of America's most blatant works of vanity. It depicts Washington, Jefferson, Lincoln, and some guy with glasses who happened to be President when it was built.

The Arc de Triomphe was intended as a monument to French vanity, but the Germans seem to have had the most use of it. Then there's the Great Wall of China, the only manmade structure large enough to be visible with the naked eye from the moon (according to the *Weekly Reader*). Nevertheless, it was all in vain and didn't stop a single Mongol.

Out in the middle of a barren plain in central Iraq stand the ruins of the largest enclosed city the world had known until the wall went up around West Berlin. Twenty-five hundred years ago Babylon was surrounded by four separate walls totaling 107 feet in thickness. They are over 70 feet in height. And along them are 360 watchtowers, one every 160 feet, to give you an idea of how long the walls are.

It contained a whole complex of palaces and the Tower of Babel, 288 feet on a side and the same in height. An estimated 58 million bricks went into the tower's construction. The walls were also of brick. Even today, dozens of towns in the area are built of Nebuchadnezzar's bricks, as is a modern dam across the Euphrates.

There are hundreds of lesser cities twenty to sixty feet beneath the clay of the Middle East, made of untold billions of bricks, kiln-baked to indestructibility in ovens fueled with charcoal and made from wood, which comes from trees, all in a land that is today completely devoid of anything even remotely resembling a forest.

I wonder if the archeologists sifting

through the parched dust of Mesopotamia or Palestine ever wonder where the millions of people it took to build these wonders got their food or why they built giant cities in the middle of the desert.

The answer is that the Near East wasn't desert 2,500 years ago. The pillars of Greece and Rome are imitations in stone of the tree trunks that were originally plentiful building material. The plains of Iraq were once as fertile as the plains of Iowa. First they cut down the forests, then they plowed the fields and used up the soil. With the trees gone, the rains came less frequently. The fields went to pasture, were overgrazed, drought followed, and erosion removed the topsoil. Herds of camels and sheep compacted the subsoil, and finally— voila!—permanent desert.

The climax ecosystem of human-populated land seems to be desert. The same process is in various stages of development all around the world. Fortunately, I like desert, but most people would put it last on their list of vacation spots. The deserts of the world don't care much for people either, and now that you know how a good many of them were made, it's hard to blame them. Many were once lush forests or grasslands, enriched by an infinitely complex variety of flora and fauna playing out the graceful cycles of life eternal.

No wonder so many desert plants are bitter, with thorns, spines, or toxic sap. You see what they got for playing Mr. Nice Guy to humanity and his friends. The wonders of the ancient world are nothing compared to desertification, without question the greatest achievement of our species.

Modern man has his own monuments to vanity. We have the Hair Club for men. (Incidentally, isn't it about time they opened it up to women?) We also have rockets. Some of them are huge, and their shape is a definite manifestation of man's ego. Actually, that's the shape men were attempting to achieve when they built the Pyramids, but stone was just too bulky. The Titan rocket is the biggest we ever built here in the United States. It's impressive.

This rocket took us all the way to the moon. Those who don't understand vanity often ask, "Why?" Who knows, really? Maybe JFK wanted to impress one of his secretaries. Maybe he just wanted to make Khrushchev look bad. When we got to the moon, you might imagine the magnitude of space would have humbled us. If nothing else, the enormity of our achievement should have made us a little less insecure. After all, it was the greatest leap of life since the amphibians hit the beach in the Paleozoic era.

But the insufferable arrogance of humanity was revealed with the very first words spoken from the surface of the moon. Twelve needlessly cruel words.

"It's one small step for a man, one giant leap for mankind," crowed Neil Armstrong, as the television audience cheered.

Right. As if the rest of the ecosystem had nothing to do with it. Not a mention of the plants that made the oxygen that fired the rockets. No "thank you" to the Cretaceous mollusks that laid down the continents one stinking shell at a time.[*]

If I were another link in the food chain, I'd have taken it as a deliberate snub. At the very least, Mr. Armstrong could have thrown a bone to the invertebrates that backed us up when we were nobodies.

"One small step for a man, one giant leap for mankind." Yeah, thanks a lot. I doubt if Neil Armstrong even wrote it himself. It sounds more like Neil Diamond.

_____
[*] Without a government contract.

Perhaps it isn't fair to castigate Neil Armstrong for mouthing banalities in his moment of triumph. After all, he was the first man to walk on the moon. But when you think about it, just about anyone can walk on the moon when it's right down at the bottom of the stairs. What's the big deal?

Not as many people remember the rest of the guys on that mission. Take Michael Collins, who piloted the orbiter that waited for the landing pod. Hardly anyone knows his name anymore. You have to feel sorry for him. Here's a man who traveled 240,000 miles to make history and then had to wait in the car.

But he shouldn't feel too bad. Who can remember the name of a single one of the Sherpas who humped Sir Edmund Hillary and all his luggage up to the top of Mount Everest?* I wonder if he promised them equal mention in the press releases? Maybe he had to bribe the Sherpas not to tell about all the times they climbed up there for fun when they were kids.

Most men today seek to express their vanity

---

* Other than Tenzing Norgay.

through technological works. But some are more privileged. Look at a dollar bill some time and you'll notice the signature on the bottom of the front side. It usually reads "James W. Baker III, Secretary of the Treasury." Now that is true vanity. As if the money is no good without his personal O.K. Not to mention the "III." The third? I beg to differ that he's only the third James Baker. I know four myself. Where does he get off calling himself Number III?

Trying to get famous by putting your name on things is irresistible to a vain man. It's not always a good idea, though.

Take the case of Thomas Crapper. He invented the flush valve, commonly used on indoor toilets, which were a novelty at the time. He named his valve after himself. The Crapper Valve.

Instead of going to the outhouse, people began installing "Crappers." Soon they were using the Crapper. It was considered a polite if somewhat technical euphemism. But the name sounds like a noun derived from a verb, so it was soon shortened to "I'm going to take a crap." His name has now entered our language. It's the root of an adjective, a noun, a verb, an expletive. You name it, you can call it crap.

So it's nice to know that vanity, hard

work, and naming everything after yourself occasionally get the reward they deserve. Now, if you'll excuse me, I've got to go take a Trump. The Shuttle, that is. See you in Washington.

PART TWO

America
and
The Big Picture

3

Declare Yourself

THE SMOKE of the Indian council fires is drifting down the winds of history, and the Great Spirit watches over 250 million people from every corner of the earth, now the most powerful, prosperous, astounding assemblage of talent and goods the world has ever known.

In a mere 200 years we have surpassed the mightiest works of the last 10,000. The interstate highway system alone makes the famed Roman roads look like cow paths. The man who built the Taj Mahal never saw an ice cube. Genghis Khan never made a phone call. Charlemagne couldn't read. Something came into being here in America, something new. America has permanently enlarged The Big Picture.

*   *   *

Everyone knows that 1987 was the two hundredth anniversary of the Constitution.* The Constitution is an amazing piece of work. Sure, you can quibble over the spelling or complain that all the s's look like f's, not to mention that it is littered with vague ambiguities and archaic language. But to me, and to a lot of people, these are not defects. I like to think of them as loopholes.

For example, the First Amendment not only guarantees the freedom to speak freely, but also the freedom to speak with your mouth full. Certainly there are limits. You can't yell "Fire" in a crowded movie theater if there's no fire. On the other hand, if there is a fire, there's no law that says you have to say anything about it. More important, you have the right to give away the end of the movie.

The Constitution has taken us to power and wealth unimaginable to those who wrote it. It has brought liberty, peace, and even happiness to millions upon millions upon millions of hopeful immigrants, and untold millions more strive to fulfill the promise it contains.

---

* And by everyone I mean one out of a hundred high school graduates.

You could call it a deed for human dignity, although if you did you would sound as if you were pontificating and people would accuse you of quoting me.

The first indications that there was something new on the earth can be found in our original contract with the world, the Declaration of Independence. We created it, and, even more, it created us. Without it, there would be no America, no Wright brothers, no Edison, no Martin Luther King, no Dean Martin, no Rowan and Martin, no martini. No one to beat Hitler, no one to go to the moon. No Hollywood, no rock or jazz, no nuclear bombs. Without the Declaration, there would only be . . . Canada.

There are those who will say, "Well, that doesn't sound so bad. The subway would be cleaner, the children could read, and slavery would have ended in 1820. Other than that, everything would be about the same."

So what was so important to our founding fathers, wealthy, middle-aged, fat and happy fellows with plenty to lose, that would make them sign that petition? What principle would make them take on the uncontested ruler of the greatest empire in their world?

They didn't do it lightly. They were scared. You can tell by reading it. The last sentence is, "And for the support of this declaration, with a firm reliance on the protection of Divine Providence, we mutually pledge to each other our lives, our fortunes and our sacred honor." That is quite a pledge. I'd trust it over the Pledge of Allegiance the same way I would trust a patriot over a politician, but we're not likely to hear it from the floor of either House anytime soon. I guess they're saving it in case the British attack again.

But that's how we started, as old Benjamin Franklin said when he signed it: "We must all hang together, or assuredly we shall all hang separately."

Besides being beautifully written, the Declaration of Independence is totally original in concept and form. It begins, "When, in the course of human events, it becomes necessary for one people to dissolve the political bands which have connected them with another, and to assume, among the powers of the earth, the separate and equal station to which the laws of nature and of nature's God entitle them, a decent respect to the opinions of mankind requires that they should declare the causes which impel them to the separation."

This is just to say that when you have a

Revolution, you owe it to the world to say *why*. This is just plain good manners. These days, the masses just shoot their dictator and take over the radio station. "A decent respect to the opinions of mankind" was something that nobody gave much thought to in that era of autocratic rule by divine right. Kings did what they damn well pleased, and mankind wasn't supposed to have an opinion. Our Founding Fathers' concern with this seemingly unimportant nicety has proven farsighted. It was public opinion that freed Eastern Europe in 1989, and it was respect for the consequences of such opinion that stopped the Soviets from sending in the tanks. These days, the power of mass electronic media has made public opinion a mighty force, and there are only a few backward governments that are not constrained in their actions by a decent respect for the opinions of mankind.*

"We hold these truths to be self-evident—that all men are created equal."

I think they held it to be self-evident because they couldn't come up with any other evidence. I sure haven't found any in my short life. But God bless them for saying it. I

---

* They are being brought into line even as I write this.

also note that they didn't say what all men are created equal *to*. Certainly not to each other. They certainly didn't mean equal to *women*. Don't forget that many of the men who signed that document held slaves; surely they didn't consider themselves equal to *them*. Since ours was the first state to remove God from every aspect of government, I sort of suspect they meant all men are created equal to God.

"That they are endowed by their Creator with certain inalienable rights; that among these are life, liberty, and the pursuit of happiness."

What!? Now life and liberty were fairly reasonable for the era. Well, life at least. Liberty was asking a little much from a divine monarch. But the pursuit of *happiness*? It was unheard of. Vague, ambiguous, all-encompassing, completely out of left field.

It was something no one had ever even requested before, let alone asserted as a God-given right. And these were merely *among* the inalienable rights men were endowed with, not even all of them. This was too much for the British. I doubt they even read further, but just started loading their muskets and getting on the boat.

Incredibly, we won those rights, and we

have defended them in a number of wars. Of course, these rights do not apply to anyone serving in the military, as anyone who has served will attest. The protection of those freedoms depends on this loophole.

Eventually, after winning liberty, those who didn't lose their lives tackled the frontier. Just when things began to get settled, they discovered they had a Manifest Destiny. After that, there was a Civil War and then a Panic, then a World War, then a Depression, then another World War.

Finally, in the early fifties, Americans began pursuing happiness. That's when I came along, by my good fortune.

4

The Road to
the Shining City
on the Hill

I WAS BORN IN 1952. I was named A. Whitney
Brown. People always ask me what the "A"
stands for, but it doesn't stand for anything.
Actually it's a form of junior. It stands for
"another." But people just call me Whitney.

Except my father. My father calls me
"Woody." You see, he wanted to name me
after Woody Guthrie, but the folks on my
mother's side were Republicans, and they

couldn't pronounce Woody Guthrie. In a smoke-filled room, the two sides compromised on "Whitney."

I came in with Eisenhower, and like most Americans I didn't think much about the rest of the world. The Big Picture was narrated by Walter Cronkite. We felt at home in the twentieth century, not knowing that a good part of the world didn't even call it that. To the Chinese, it was the Year of the Dragon in the thirty-sixth century. To the Arabs it was the year 566. The Jews called it the fifty-seventh century. The Hebrew calendar is the oldest in the world, but maybe the Jews have better accounting methods. On the other hand, they don't lose track of time whenever God appears in the flesh.

It was a different world in the fifties. There were no salad bars. Even when people started doing their own thing in the sixties they never imagined they would end up making their own salads in the seventies. Salad itself was in a very primitive stage of evolution at the time. It was just a little sprig of parsley on the side of the plate. Fish were cooked in my childhood. Even Jules Verne didn't predict sushi, God rest his soul. Pasta was called noodles. It was a simpler world.

The Heimlich maneuver hadn't even been dreamed of yet. People were choking to death left and right in steak houses all over the country. On well-done steaks, for the most part, because there was no rare west of the Hudson.

There were no herpes and no AIDS, but you couldn't have caught them if there had been. People had morals then, and morals were highly defined. They knew right from wrong in those days. They still did plenty of wrong, but they felt guilty about it afterward. Everything was black and white, except blacks. They were colored.

I remember when I was eight or nine and my family took a trip to Lookout Mountain, Tennessee. I don't know why. We hadn't burned up enough gas that week I guess, and the neighbors were starting to talk. At the summit there was a little Indian souvenir stand. You could buy whooping crane feather dusters and condor wishbones—stuff like that. I bought this little toy tomtom drum. When I got it home, I noticed that it said "Made in Japan" on the bottom.

In the sixties everything began to change, and fast. Part of the change was the civil rights movement, part of it the peace movement, some of it was drugs and sex. We were drunk with the dizziness of full freedom (to quote some existential philosopher, I forget who—they were so common back then), and we were seeing double standards wherever we looked.

The death of John Kennedy hit us in the face like a bucket of cold water from the bottomless well of disillusionment. It jerked the rug out from under our ordered, optimistic view of the universe. It made our own patriotism seem hollow and that of others jingoistic.

"Ask not what your country can do for you; ask what you can do for your country," JFK had admonished us.

When we asked the question at all, it was a rhetorical expression of futility: "Hey, man, what can *I* do?"

Walt Whitman said, "Not a grave of the martyred for freedom but sprouts the seeds of freedom." But it was only stunted weeds of cynicism that grew in the light of the eternal flame.

I became cynical so quickly after President Kennedy was killed that by the time I heard that Governor Connally had also been wounded, it hardly seemed to matter.

In The Big Picture, the senseless red stains

of November 1963 can now be seen as the strokes of the Master Artist. An intricate and beautiful design on a clashing background of black and white. Because it was only Lyndon Baines Johnson who could have passed the Civil Rights Act through Congress.

The Boll Weevil Democrats could and would have held up civil rights and voting rights for nearly a decade against any Harvard liberal who tried to cram them down their throats. Johnson was a Southerner, and he had the killer instincts of a fine coon dog. He took no shit from the good ole boys. He left them nowhere to run and nowhere to hide.

Kennedy illuminated the White House with culture, hope, and youth. He radiated grace. Johnson ruled the Senate with an iron fist. He sweated power. The only reason Kennedy was President in the first place was that Johnson stole the election from Nixon in Texas and Daley stole it from the Republicans in Chicago.

There are no erasures in The Big Picture. The Artist's work is freehand, a seeming random smear; the lives of men are colors lavished freely on his canvas. But the indelible red of martyrs' blood is the most precious on his pallet.

The destiny of Lyndon Baines Johnson

was marked with it, and it left him few choices. He was the one who had to keep the promises John Kennedy had made. In life, Kennedy didn't have to prove himself. He was born a hero. Eloquent, handsome, his ideals were impeccably lofty, his liberalism above suspicion. He could afford to promise and compromise.

Johnson had to deliver. He was no golden boy; he was the booby prize for a nation robbed of its radiant Apollo. No achievement could make him worthy of our devotion, but no one else could have passed the Civil Rights Act, the Voting Rights Act, the Water Quality Act, to name a few. When his job was done in 1968, he quit and retired to his ranch to smoke and eat. Five years later he was dead, may he rest in peace.

As for me, I discovered acid in the summer of '68, and subsequently took enough to do chromosome damage to a Buick. For most of the winter of '68–'69 I stumbled through a psychedelic blizzard. I became a shiftless teenage derelict, hitchhiking from Dead concert to Dead concert, trying to see through my hair.

Through the white haze I could make out a strange roaring sound. I was told later it was the babble of that great deaf mute of history, the Silent Majority, articulating its choice for President, Richard Milhous Nixon.

Most of my generation didn't have a clue to what was going on. In fact, we greeted each other with the very question: "What's going on, man?"

We didn't say, "Nice to see you" or "How have you been?" as people do when they have a value system that isn't crumbling in front of their eyes.

We wanted to know, "What's happening, brother? What's the deal, dude? What's the buzz, man?" Nobody knew.

The only answer I ever got was, "What it is." What it was, I never heard.

The search for meaning came naturally to me. I grew up in a generation so starved for understanding we were able to read significance into Donovan lyrics.

We all read *Siddhartha*. It was a book about Buddha. The story of a guy who found the true path by trying everything. He reached wisdom by the process of elimination. It took him a long time.

But I must say he had fewer things to try than we did. His was not exactly a happening age. In our times, even if he had made it through drugs, music, and sex, he could easily have gotten wrapped up in social change or a good cause. The search for a more just society today would turn a thousand Buddhas into burned-out bureaucrats.

Christ himself would have been lucky to make it past EST seminar training with his immortal soul intact. Mohammed would no doubt have lost the notes for his Holy Koran in a fire caused by an Israeli raid on the apartment next door and spent his middle years bogged down in factional infighting within the PLO.

Moses would still have been a shepherd, but he would have had 4,000 acres under lease from the Department of the Interior.

Like many, I set out to find myself, but I soon realized that was a little too ambitious, since most of the time I was lucky if I could find my shoes.

By 1969 I was picking up cigarette butts in the streets of Flagstaff. I wasn't concerned with geopolitical affairs, international events, historical perspectives, or hygiene.

Then one day, one fine day, I found an extralong Viceroy butt. It wasn't what I had set off searching for on my quest for meaning, but it was in mint condition, barely smoked.

I took it back to the dumpster where I was living at the time and kicked back to cele-brate, eating some coffee grounds my mother had loaned me for my birthday, thinking to myself, "Things just don't get any better than this."

There was a toothless Indian alcoholic who lived in the dumpster with me. I let him stay there because he watched the place while I was gone. He'd pulled all his teeth out when he was a kid, figuring to get moncy from the tooth fairy. When she never showed, he got bitter and turned to drink.

I looked at him there, the last remnant of a once proud and hopeful race of Ancient Americans, completely seduced by the glit-ter and tinsel of civilization. They say you can judge a man by the way he reacts when the culture that's nourished him and his people for thousands of years collapses in his lifetime. He was doing about as well as I was.

I identified with him. My culture, too, had failed me. I needed answers, and he was the only one who would listen to my questions.

I grabbed him by the forelock and said, "Rafael, what happened to you? Your peo-ple used to be somebody on this continent.

Did a maniac kill your chief? Was it drugs? What was it, man?"

"I had a souvenir stand on Lookout Mountain," he muttered.

"I was there," I said. "I could see seven states."

For a moment his eyes cleared and I saw him again as he once was, a proud young brave, riding his wild pony at full gallop across the K Mart parking lot in the land of his birth. In his voice was the strength of the northwest wind.

"The white man is like the grass that covers vast prairies. The red man resembles the scattered trees of a storm-swept plain."

"I know," I said. "But at least you got to name everything. What more do you want?"

"The land," he told me.

"I'm sorry," I said. "But you'll never get the land back. We have it in writing."

"My people are this land," he intoned. "The very earth upon which you walk every day is made from the dust of my ancestors' bones." His voice was quiet, infused with simple pride.

"They were simple mollusks," he went on. "And they had calciferous shells. Some of them were bivalves, some of them were gastropods."

It was true, I knew.

"They were peace-loving folk with a sedimentary life-style," he explained, almost apologetically.

Outside the noise of the traffic grew muffled, like the bellowing of buffalo moving over the plains in countless numbers. Suddenly the sky darkened and the earth shook. I realized they were emptying the dumpster.

5

How Ronald Reagan and Pot Are Related

WHEN THE starry-eyed social activism of the sixties glazed over into the squinting cynicism of the seventies, my generation was left peeping through the keyhole of the Me Decade into the darkness of the future. Like burned-out moths, we were drawn to that circle of limited brilliance cast by the cheerful candle of neoconservatism.

We still wanted to make the world a better place, but now only for those who could afford it, and it turned out it was a rare ex-hippie who wouldn't turn Republican if you promised him a few bucks off his taxes. What's more, he'd believe he was getting it.

It was hippies who paved the way for the Reagan Revolution because it was pot that made the symptoms of senility socially acceptable. It's hard to believe Ronnie was only sixty-nine when we elected him way back in 1980.

As for the Reagan legacy, what can you say about a President who cites the invasion of Grenada as the greatest accomplishment of his administration? Except that, well, I agree with that assessment.

It may not seem like much for the greatest military power the world has ever known to knock over a fruit stand with two aircraft carriers, but sometimes you have to put your foot down.

If it happens to be on the smallest country in your hemisphere, so much the better. He deserves some credit for even finding a country we could whip. Nineteen Americans lost their lives in Grenada, half, it now appears, by the guns of their own trigger-happy comrades.*

But the goal was more emotional than strategic—to restore U.S. pride—and the greatest tragedy, besides the dead soldiers, was that it worked. A wave of patriotism gripped the country like a pit bull on a pork roast.

Operations like these occasionally have to be done in the world of real politics, but it's not something you go around bragging about later. Even the Russians had enough class not to smirk after they invaded Afghanistan.

But I guess it was a success, and you have to admit the invasion's impact will be felt long after Reagan's other great achievement, the Catastrophic Health Plan, which was repealed fifteen months after he signed it—especially in the context of the times. Times when a hit-and-run driver could wipe out 241 of our finest peacekeepers in Beirut. When cocaine was dropping from 60,000 dollars a kilo to 8,000, making it possible for thousands of teenagers to enter the business world standing lookout for crack dealers and

---

* If you take into account all the medical students practicing medicine in unsuspecting communities all over the country, the toll may be much higher.

selling Uzis to their little brothers. Times when we were squandering a half century of economic superiority to build lasers in the sky with borrowed Japanese money to protect our right to be the world's largest debtor.

Grenada wasn't America's only military triumph of the eighties. There was also the Gulf of Sidra maneuvers. Plenty of glory there. Crossing an imaginary line—now that's something to stand up and crow about.

The great thing about attacking Libya, besides the fact that it always deserves it, is you don't have to worry about any other country leaping to its defense. No country in the college of civilized nations wants to align itself with the class twit. I suppose that's why we attacked Libya in retaliation for the bombing of that disco in West Berlin when in fact it was the Syrians (with the collaboration of East Germany) who were responsible. You have to admit it seems to have quieted Qaddafi down a bit, though. (Knock on wood.)

Let's not forget the tax cuts, now *there* is a legacy we can all bank on. But be honest, how many of you actually saved any of it? Really, did anybody put a penny of it away?

No. We blew it all on . . . Sonys, Hondas, Nikons, BMWs, Perrier, Chivas, Dos Equis. It seemed there was nothing a foreign country could produce that we wouldn't buy. We bought stuff we couldn't even pronounce. Let's see, were the tax cuts anywhere near our trade deficit? Essentially we stopped paying for the services we demanded of our government and spent the money on luxury goods, mostly from Japan, which then loaned us the money back to make up for what we weren't paying in taxes, at 10 percent, like an agent's commission. Japan was only too happy to do so, because it kept the whole circle in operation.

When things got tight and the federal government needed even more money, it cut services to the states and cities and in turn raised taxes to make up for it. When that wasn't enough it raised Social Security taxes and threw the funds into general revenue. As income taxes went down, all the other ones went up. Taxes were never cut, they just became more regressive.

Reagan left his mark on the Supreme Court as well, if not his Bork. And I have only sympathy for Douglas Ginsburg, even though it's all for the best he won't be a Supreme Court justice. I'm not questioning his qualifications, it's just that every time his last name came up, you'd have to ask, "The poet or the judge?" and it would be too much hassle.

Still, I think the Reagan administration should get some credit for creativity on that one. I mean where did he even find a Jewish hard-line conservative Republican pot smoker? He sounds like an Oprah Winfrey guest.

The hilarious uproar of betrayed conservatives was tempered for me by the implication that if casual pot use in one's past was a disqualification for high appointive office, my entire generation was locked out of the halls of power along with him.

As far as foreign policy during the Reagan era went, well, the Gipper pretty much left the remnants of American credibility scattered around Tehran like pork-chop bones at a Baptist picnic.

Of course, there are stupider things than running guns to Iran. Say, setting your sister up on a blind date with Ted Bundy. The fact is that the Great Communicator just couldn't resist the opportunity to get a couple of hostages out before Election Day and Khomeini set Reagan up like a gringo tourist.

Then Reagan was shocked at the double cross. Why didn't he just buy a Rolex in

Times Square and call it a day? We ended up with a worldwide sideshow with us as the freaks, courtesy of Ayatollah Khomeini, the P. T. Barnum of the Shiite circus whose motto was: In the U.S. there's a hostage born every minute.

This is what happens when you turn your foreign policy over to a guy named "Bud": Bud McFarlane, our goodwill ambassador to Tehran, bearing Bibles and cakes. The Iranians probably didn't know which one to eat first. This was a guy who should have been turning back Datsun odometers at a car lot in Jersey, even though in the end he did indeed turn out to be Honest Bud McFarlane, with a tear in his eye and a legal bill he can never pay, whimpering that someone had set him up.

The least the Reagan administration could have done is get some simple-minded civilian to take the fall like they did in Nicaragua. Remember Hasenfus, the guy who was shot down in a coke runner's plane full of guns over Nicaragua with George Bush's phone number in his wallet? He would have been perfect for the Iranian gig. What a brilliant defense he mounted in Managua— "Don't blame me, I was only in it for the money."

*   *   *

Balancing these errors in an objective and statesmanlike manner, it must be said that Ronald Reagan did live up to his promise to "get government off the backs of the people." "People," of course, meaning defense contractors, chemical manufacturers, stockbrokers, high-living Savings and Loan officers, and cocaine wholesalers.

It's a matter of record that never during either campaign did Reagan specifically say he considered students, workers, the poor, the old, the blind, AIDS patients, small farmers, city dwellers, nature lovers, or liberals to be people.

And even if he did, he may have been misquoted. What he actually said was that he would "get government to turn its back on the people." Although some of his advisers have sworn they heard "Get to the government trough when the people turn their backs."

He did get those parasitic air traffic controllers off the backs of airline passengers. I can't tell you what a relief that is every time I strap myself in for a takeoff or a landing even now, after eight years.

But one thing should be straightened out. Reagan and Bush both denounced Carter because the Soviet invasion of Afghanistan happened "on his watch." The invasion

ended up a quagmire of nightmare propor-
tions that finally turned the Soviet people
against the militaristic daydreams of their
doddering leadership.

Afghanistan was the last straw for the
Russian masses, and it helped create the cli-
mate for *perestroika* and *glasnost*. So Jimmy
Carter deserves some of the credit for the
collapse of communism. He let the communists buy the rope they hung themselves
with.*

I think, in a way, Nancy Reagan was more
style than substance. I mean, compared to
other first ladies in my lifetime. "Just say
no" is a great slogan, but if you can't it's
nice to know you can check into the Betty
Ford Clinic. Or check your horoscope and
know she's checking hers at the very same
moment. Or sober up while reading her riv-
eting best-seller with the frightening title
My Turn.

Maybe I missed the point, but to me the
most memorable part of the Reagan legacy
will be those medical diagrams of his colon
polyps.

I admit I got a little teary-eyed when I

---

* Lenin: "They will sell us the rope we hang them
with."

heard the old guy mumbling on about "The Shining City on the Hill," even though all the best buildings are owned by Japanese bankers now.

In our search for the true legacy of the Reagan Revolution, it would be all too easy to say it amounts to nothing more than a few years of euphoric delusion followed by embarrassment and crass commercialism.

But nothing exposes it better than our former President's first trip abroad after he left office. Never one to align himself with a bunch of losers, he headed straight for Japan. While Gorbachev was in Eastern Europe, eloquently espousing the cause of openness and self-determination for the countries behind the Iron Curtain, Ronald Reagan was kowtowing to our corporate competitors and pimping his presidential prestige to the highest bidder.

It's humiliating that an ex-President of the great United States has a part-time job peddling the products of a foreign country. It demeans the presidency, if that's still possible. Say what you want about Stalin, at least he didn't do commercials.

This is the man who promised to make America stand tall again. Why doesn't he just join a carnival and set up a "Dunk the American President" booth? Three throws for a quarter. He could make a fortune at fifty yards anywhere in the Third World.

I don't think any of us expected the man who played the Gipper to emerge as an elder statesman. I pictured him melting into a pool chair in Bel Air, haranguing his Nicaraguan lawn boy about the evils of bilingualism. I guess that was a little too dignified for Reagan.

He had to go on the Fujisankei network in Japan to say how wonderful it was that Sony gobbled up Columbia Pictures because maybe the Japanese can bring some class back to Hollywood. I guess that means the Japanese are going to release *Mothra* on Beta.

He was paid $2 million for two speeches during that trip. But you won't hear me criticizing Reagan for overcharging them. They got him cheap, when you figure that his "Star Wars" speech alone must have cost us $200 billion, minimum.

Besides the $2 million speaking fee, Fuji also donated a few million for the Reagan library. He's actually going to build one. Apparently he needs a place to preserve all those papers he never got around to reading.

I don't doubt it'll be a real magnet for scholars in the future. I picture it as a split-level stucco warehouse with rows of *Read-*

er's Digest Condensed Books and a mag-
nifying glass by every chair.

At least the Japanese got their money's
worth. On the other hand, they didn't elect
him, which is probably why they could afford to hire him.

Anyway, as Ronald Reagan rides off into the
sunset, I wish him the best. There's no one
I'd rather see live to a healthy, ripe old age,
except maybe Thurgood Marshall.

In The Big Picture show, he made us
laugh, he made us cry. He brought the magic
of Hollywood to the drab world of presidential politics. It's only natural the Reagan
magic turned out to be exactly like the
magic of film: a still picture with the illu-
sion of motion.

6

How Maple Syrup Elects Our Presidents

WHEN OUR FOREFATHERS created the office of President it probably seemed like a good idea at the time. After all, the woods were full of leaders of presidential timber. In those days, all you had to do was vote for the man you liked the most and forget about it for four years.

But then sometime around the Tyler campaign, it degenerated into the lesser of two evils. You had to vote for the man you disliked the least. Now, it's come to the point where you have to vote against the man you dislike the most.

No matter how much you liked Reagan, the spotlight of history shows that he was not as brilliant as Richard Nixon. I think it may eventually show he was not as honest, either. And the time will come when we will say Jimmy Carter looked good. It may have already come, now that we need Egypt for some other reason than to consume our surplus wheat.

Our chief executives seem to be declining in stature. Maybe our soil is becoming depleted, and some essential leadership nutrient is lacking, or maybe our diet is too rich. It happened to the French.

Some people blame the media for the low quality of our candidates, but the press was pretty truthful this past campaign. Television, in particular, had commendably balanced coverage of the battle. In all of today's electoral bouts, TV has become the referee. For the most part it has been impartial, which is not surprising, considering that it's also nearsighted, has a minuscule attention span, and spends the entire fight selling peanuts to the spectators.

Besides, there are so many liars in the

news during election years that the press doesn't have any room for its own lies. I have nothing against lying in general—after all, I work on television. It's just incompetent lying I object to. I don't want an honest President any more than anyone else; there are some hard facts out there I'd rather not face right now. The best we can hope for, and in fact the most we deserve, is a liar we can believe in.

Unfortunately, I don't think we are ever going to have a great liar to lead us in the near future because there is just too much scrutiny of the candidates. When you enter elementary school, your teacher tells you everything you do wrong will go into your permanent record. This is to put you on your best behavior. After a few years, most people catch on that this threat is greatly exaggerated. If you expose yourself during recess in the first grade, usually by the time you graduate from law school, you will have come to terms with the antisocial demons who goaded you into that act. Provided you don't do it again, society will soon forget.

You can vote, get a driver's license, hold a job, even marry and have children, and no one will be the wiser. You can even become a mayor or a congressman. But if you run for President or are selected for the Supreme

Court, you can count on that early act becoming a topic in a national debate. Some reporter might even win a Pulitzer Prize for digging it up.

The simple fact is, lying takes a while to master; even the best make mistakes early in their careers. A presidential aspirant can expect every one of those mistakes to be exposed, and that's a shame. Just because he was a bad liar once doesn't mean he hasn't grown.

Look at George Bush: experienced, pragmatic, and by his own account a consensus builder, which means he's willing to change if it will make us like him better. Look at his flip-flops over the budget, for example. He's fine against a two-bit piker like Noriega, and he can almost hold his own against a pretentious pontificator like Dan Rather, but only time will tell if he can stand up to a bloodthirsty, power-mad dictator like, say, John Major.

Still, what was the choice? Bob Dole was completely transparent. I thought I caught him in a lie once when he said he liked George Bush as a person, but later I realized he was just being sarcastic.

Pat Robertson was believable, if you don't believe in evolution. Gephardt had great promise. Accusing foreigners of unfairly making superior merchandise and taking our jobs is just the kind of good old American lie that made the U.S.A. number, well, whatever number we are these days. He could stand there bald-faced, and I mean literally: He had no eyebrows. There was once a time when a man like Richard Gephardt could have picnicked on protectionist pabulum all the way to the presidency, but that was way back when there were as many workers in the country as consumers.

Jesse Jackson was a special case. He was accused of bigotry by Mayor Koch early in the campaign and he said, "I not only deny the allegations, I deny the alligator." At least I think it was Jesse, it may have been the Kingfish. The Jackson campaign struck a powerful chord in the hearts of many because he carried a message of hope to the powerless, the message being that no one will question the veracity of any political statement that rhymes.

I liked Al Haig and Bruce Babbitt. One looked like a madman, and one talked like one. It cost them. Babbitt made it as far as Iowa, but it was just a matter of time before he became a victim of his Peter Finch–Network eyes, bulging into the TV cameras with wild visions of responsible solutions to complex problems. Nobody told him that primary elections are about deals, not ideals. He stood up to be counted, and someone stole his chair.

Haig went out with less than 1 percent in New Hampshire. It was the end of the dream for us Haigheads, as we called ourselves. Alex, we hardly knew ye. He was tough, Al Haig, but tender. Hard-boiled Haig, we called him. Not to his face, of course.

When it came to the general election, Dukakis made himself very hard to vote for. Physically, he never engendered trust; he had burglar shoulders. Kitty had that look of a woman on the verge of hysteria, a look most men over thirty have learned to recognize even in bar light at 2:00 A.M. You can't blame her. After Bernard Shaw asked her husband what he would do if she were raped she must have felt like an easy target.

On a gut level, a lot of Americans decided Dukakis didn't have any, but not so much on the basis of that ugly little incident. It was the way he denied being a liberal. If someone calls you a name that isn't bad, especially one that you're at liberty to define in your favor, and if instead you try to deny it, you look like a coward.

We're still left with the question of why anyone would want to put him- or herself through the process. What kind of a principled man would put up with eighteen months of cowering and begging to a faceless bunch of ill-informed, media-degenerated John Q. common denominators? For what, so he can tell his friends he got elected President?

The candidate has to totally abase himself by sucking up to one of the least analytic and most self-deluded electorates in the world, and then we expect him to be respected around the world by leaders who took power through brute strength or Machiavellian cunning. It's a lot to ask.

One of the main bottlenecks in our electoral process is New Hampshire. Every election, it gets first cut. Its inhabitants pass themselves off as some kind of Normal Rockwell poobahs. Well, my question is, who died and made them kingmakers? It just isn't fair. If the primaries were all at the same time my apartment building could vote as a bloc and cancel out the state's entire electoral body.

"The Granite State"—it has a solid, permanent sound to it. A more accurate name would be "The Small Mammals by the Side of the Road State." "Live Free or Die," that's their motto. That's what it says on their license plates. But when you consider that those license plates are made in prison it makes you wonder how sincere it is.

I always thought of it as a threat . . . live free or die. But from the few times I've visited New Hampshire, as far as I can tell it's a reference to how cheap they are.

I don't mean to come down so hard on the state, I just feel a little leery about handing the future of our government over to a bunch of people I wouldn't even ask the time of day from. And a lot of these people are farmers. You can always tell by the hat. I know, because I have farmers in my family. Now don't get me wrong, farmers are good people. They love their crops and all, but they don't get out much.

Those that aren't farmers are truck drivers. Dwell on that for a moment; minutes after eating truck-stop food, these people are in the booth voting. As if that weren't frightening enough, I'll tell you something else about New Hampshire people: they get up early.

They're morning people. Do we want morning people choosing the candidates for the highest office in the free world? Morning people have a disturbing tendency to tyranny, as you know if you've ever lived with one. It's a known fact that every major dictator in history was a morning person.

Maybe I'm wrong. Maybe it's perfectly safe to place the destiny of our nation in the hands of a pack of maple-syrup-swilling squirrel worshippers. It just seems a little risky considering that hundreds of thousands of brave men, many of them night owls and slugabeds, died for our right to vote.

Actually that's a bit of a myth; the only ones who actually died for that right were those who died in the Revolutionary War, and possibly the War of 1812, or, as it is known in Canada, the War of Annexation. Also those who died at the Alamo, to bring Texas into the Union, and some of Frémont's men who died in California. The Midwest and south-central states we bought from Napoleon, and Alaska was purchased from Russia without loss of life or limb, although it did cost Secretary of State Seward his reputation as a fiscal conservative.

During the Civil War voting was in question only for Southern blacks, and the Spanish American War was to annex Cuba and the Philippines because William Randolph Hearst thought America wouldn't be complete without a few colonies. World War I was to save the French right to change governments every few weeks and the British right to have a queen. We entered World War II because Japan tried to take Hawaii without paying for it. Our right to vote was never in question at any time. We haven't worked or fought as hard for that right as we would like ourselves to believe, and our voter turnout is the lowest in the democratic world.

Most Americans love their country very dearly. But a lot of men love their wives dearly too, and yet they sit there in front of the TV with a beer and a bag of pork rinds and don't even notice her getting old as the years go by. Sound like our President?

To coin a metaphor, the orgasm of democracy is voting. All the passions come to climax in that booth. Yet in America half the body politic can't even get it up.

It's our national shame. Last year in Haiti hundreds of penniless peasants laid down their lives in brutal massacres simply for the privilege of casting a ballot. And here in the home of the brave, 40 to 60 percent of the electorate doesn't even bother to walk down the block to the polls.

Having said all this, I confess I failed to vote in the last election. Not the last presidential election, but our New York City showdown. I'm not apathetic, far from it. I'm just afraid that if I vote for a guy and then he screws up, they'll blame it on me. Besides, to just go down and vote seems sort of high-handed. I know I have the right and everything, but who am I to be passing down judgments on one and all? "*I* have anointed *you* to rule over *us*." Besides, I didn't want to risk jury duty.

7

The Bush Era

GEORGE BUSH says he wants to be known as the "Education President" and the "Environmental President." I don't know what was stopping him from being the "Education and Environmental *Vice** President." It's not as if he would have been stepping on any toes in those areas during the Reagan administration. Say what you want about George Bush's former boss, he knew how to delegate.

George Bush is famous for having a personal touch. He calls people on their birthdays. He remembers the little things. Maybe

---

* In either sense of the word.

he's the one who remembered Grenada, sitting out there in the Caribbean like a hubcap in Tijuana.

There is nothing quite like a Caribbean invasion to kick off a presidency. I mean, other than busting one of your old drug buddies in a monastery. The great thing about going after Noriega is that you have a popular target. Guatemala and Honduras and Dominica had his coca routes divvied up before the first American soldier hit the bodega. That's the way to wage a war on drugs—spread the drugs around! Latin America always gets anxious when we in the North get new weapons that need testing or have a bunch of new recruits we want to break in, but in Noriega's case they were glad to see him go. All of them except Castro. I would guess the whole scenario made Castro a little queasy.

It's one thing to invade a dictator's country and oust him from power. It has happened to most Latin American leaders at one time or another, and it's not considered dishonorable in the least. But what made the Panama operation unique was the utter humiliation served up to General Noriega. Here he was, one minute a multimillionaire strongman waving a machete, his picture in every government building. And then, sud-

denly he's cowering in a phone booth outside a Dairy Queen, or hiding out in the base-
ment of a church, his picture on the wall of
every post office.

But the real feather in Bush's Panama hat
was printing Noriega's mug shot in all the
papers, wearing a grimy T-shirt and looking
as if he were about to cry. That is just the
kind of thing people mean when they talk
about George Bush's personal touch. He
takes an interest, making sure the general's
loved ones have something to put in the
scrapbook.

I can just imagine the troop photographer
mocking poor Manuel. "Hey, Tony, show us
your good side! Whoops, sorry, that is your
good side. By the way, is that a lunar map
on your face or are you just going through a
phase?"

No question George Herbert Walker Bush
knows how to seize his moment in history.
He was inaugurated on the two hundredth
anniversary of the presidency, and he actually made it the theme of his inaugural ball.
"From George to George" was how he put it,
but if I were he I wouldn't be at such pains
to remind everybody of the fact that we
started out with Washington and ended up
with Bush. It's been a rough two hundred

years. From "I cannot tell a lie" to "I cannot tell."

I didn't make the inaugural, unfortunately. I heard it was one hell of a party, though. It's hard to believe you could have so much fun for only $30 million. I have to admit that a fun-filled, meaningless media event like the inaugural ball was a real relief after all the substantive discussion of the campaign.

I'm not begrudging Bush the right to throw a little bash; it's not every day you beat out a formidable opponent like Mike Dukakis. Thirty million seems a little excessive. (Just think, that's almost enough money to bribe the Hezbollah into releasing the hostages. In a way it's almost too bad it's morally wrong to deal with terrorists.)

In all, there were eleven inaugural balls. Now some people would say that's excessive, but it takes a lot of balls to throw a $30 million celebration before you've even done anything. People actually paid $15,000 for a hotel suite overlooking the parade. I find that silly because I happen to know you can sleep on a grate just a block from the White House for almost nothing, summer and winter. The only difference is the President won't wave to you from his limousine.

When you put it all into The Big Picture,

what's $30 million these days anyway? The crack concession across from the Executive Office Building could cover the tab in one good weekend. One other thing, I'll bet security wasn't nearly as tight at George Washington's inaugural. But then that George had John Adams for his vice president.

Until Americans got bored with the Persian Gulf crisis, President Bush had the highest approval rating in history for this point in a presidency. There's no arguing with statistics. I'm forced to admit that for a man who pandered his way into the presidency by appealing to the lowest common denominator of ignorant bigotry and knee-jerk patriotism, George Bush has actually proven to be a shapeless political jellyfish.

He opened his presidency with an attack on the Bill of Rights. He insisted there was an error in the First Amendment, knowing, as he does, the constitutional intent so much better than our Supreme Court. I'm talking about the flag brouhaha.

Only a lowlife asshole would burn the American flag, and everybody knows it. But in America, there's no law against being a lowlife asshole, and I'd like to keep it that way.

I'll tell you why. Because it's a privilege to

respect our country's banner, the same as it's a privilege to serve her. To coerce that respect from the unwilling is an egregious insult to those who give it freely. I want people to know I respect the flag because I love it, not because I'm afraid of the law. Letting two or three pathetic brats burn the flag without penalty is the only way to be sure the other 249-odd million of our fellow citizens honor it from their hearts.

Besides, I'm instinctively against any law I wouldn't break if I could get away with it. It's bad enough there's a federal law against burning money. The government got around that by deregulating Savings and Loans.*

Consider the implications of this seemingly harmless law. It would mean that by simply not burning the flag I would become a law-abiding citizen. I don't like the sound of it. First thing you know I'd be hanging around with informed constituents and civic-minded individuals. Pretty soon I'd become a defensive driver, a responsible consumer, and an honest taxpayer, maybe even a concerned parent. That's how people end up as innocent bystanders.

It just isn't my crowd. I'm more at home with irate customers, difficult patients,

---

* Flags aren't insured.

heedless pedestrians, and unreliable witnesses. These are the real Americans: embit-
tered veterans, disgruntled employees, noisy
neighbors, Monday morning quarterbacks,
inconsiderate smokers, apathetic voters, in-
different sales clerks.

Just don't accuse us of disrespecting the
men and women who gave their lives for
their country, except maybe the idiots who
volunteered for the Spanish American War.
It's often been said in this debate that many
brave Americans died for our flag. That is
certainly true, but it's equally true that a lot
of cowards died for it, too. They deserve to
be remembered just as much, perhaps even
more, because a coward dies a thousand
deaths and a brave man dies but once. Even
more people have died following stupid or-
ders they weren't allowed to speak out
against.

We've had constitutional amendments
that freed entire races of people. Now, I'm
not saying the President has better things to
do. I know he has his hands full selling the
national forests to Japanese sawmills and
auctioning ambassadorships at party fund-
raisers, but it makes me wish flag smoke is
what's causing all this acid rain.

The Bill of Rights is the masterpiece of
some of the best minds of the Age of Enlight-

enment. Old Glory isn't even Betsy Ross's best work.* At least twenty-nine different countries have red, white, and blue flags. It's not exactly what you would call a ground-breaking concept in the world of flag design.

It's easy to get a symbol mixed up with what it stands for. I know this because when I was a teenager I used to sleep with a *Playboy* magazine. It was only a picture, but to me it was a symbol of sex. I suppose to some people a photo opportunity at a flag factory is a symbol of freedom. But to me they're both just jerking off.

Any reasonable, open-minded Democrat would conclude that this whole battle began with the Reagan Revolution, but for once, I'm sorry to say, he would be mistaken. It's older than that, believe it or not. There was even a time when people were burned instead of flags, just for *thinking* about putting their faith in a symbol. The First Commandment says, "Thou shalt not make unto thee any graven image." What is a flag but the tangible icon of our intangible freedom? We're talking about a subject that is biblical in scope.

I will not stoop so far as to accuse the

---

* She did a needlepoint of a log cabin that was just fabulous.

Republican leadership of idolatry. It's a tired, old, timeworn cliché that may have been true at one time, but it certainly no longer applies, at least not to the centrist wing of the party. Doctrinaire flag worshipping may bear some superficial resemblances to Satanic ritualism, but I think in this day and age most Republicans wouldn't dream of mixing the two. And capital-gains worship has nothing to do with communion, does it?

Still, the principle is the same; amending the Constitution to protect the flag is like amending the Bible to protect Catholic school uniforms. Soon we would be adding an Eleventh Commandment: "Thou shalt not sit on the Pope's hat."

Any country that loves freedom so much it will let its own flag be burned for the sake of it is just following the example of their God, who loved his people so much he let them kill his son.

On the other hand, it would be all too easy to point out that it certainly wouldn't *hurt* the present administration if the way things looked were more important than the way they are, but that would be delving into the realm of opinion, something I am loath to do.

* * *

In many ways this struggle between appearance and reality will decide how we live our lives and maybe whether we even survive at all. In another part of the world it's called *perestroika*. The Soviets' government lies to them, but at least no one believes those lies. Our enemy is the lies we tell ourselves, and we're more inclined to believe them.

George Bush came into office as a pragmatic consensus builder. His goal was to reach out and extend his hand to the opposition, both in his party and among the Democrats. He started out by appointing Elizabeth Dole Secretary of Transportation, making sure his bitter rival in the primaries would be present at all official functions in the role of Cabinet spouse. Like I said, he has that personal touch.

8

Bush v. *Roe* v. *Wade*

MARIO CUOMO, the governor of New York, recently declared the nineties "The Decade of the Child." It's nice to know there's at least one kid somebody is paying attention to. This year, several thousand crack babies reached the age of five and entered kindergarten in the New York public school system.

When they were born, most of them screamed in agony twenty hours a day for a couple of years. It has been demonstrated on a few of them that intensive, patient, loving intervention on a constant and long-term basis holds the possibility of turning them into normal, healthy children. It isn't easy, but it can be done, with enough dedication.

Were they to receive such care, and if it were effective and homes and parents could be found for them, and they lived a normal childhood like any kid in New York, it would raise their chances of finishing school to almost fifty-fifty. It's an exciting possibility.

So far I haven't seen anyone lying down in front of apartment buildings to protect the children's right to have breakfast before they go to school, and no one ever chains himself in the hallways of the projects to assert the right of the already born not to be shot while waiting for Mommy to wake up after school.

Nevertheless, President Bush has called on the Supreme Court to overturn *Roe* v. *Wade*. We can assume the vice president's thoughts on the subject are pretty much the same, although not as frequent or as fully formed. In fact, according to the *Washington Post* Dan Quayle thought *Roe* v. *Wade* were alternative ways to cross the Potomac.

Some say this is a political issue, but it seems to me more of a religious issue. If it's not religious, then why is it that the people making a big issue out of the rights of the unborn are always people that have been born again?

And I have a sympathy for religion because I was raised by a religious cult: the Baptists. The Baptists are a strange and little-known Protestant sect broken into two splinter groups, Northern and Southern. Each holds the other to be heretical blasphemers. Their basic theology is that if you hold someone under water long enough, he'll come around to your way of thinking. It's a ritual known as "Bobbing for Baptists."

The Baptists believe in The Right to Life before you're born. They also believe in Life After Death, but that is a privilege and you have to earn it by spending the interim in guilt-ridden misery. At an early age I decided that living a life of pious misery in hope of going to heaven when it's over is a lot like keeping your eyes shut all through a movie in the hope of getting your money back at the end.

I finally left the church, but they got even; they sent my address to the Jehovah's Witnesses. Said I wanted to be saved but my only free time was before 7:00 A.M. Five of them showed up one Sunday morning. They tried to gang-save me on the front porch.

I like babies because I have one. In addition, I was one, so I feel qualified to speak on their likes and dislikes. They don't like being born, for one thing. Poor little ignorant things. Of course I don't know that for sure, I'm just going by their facial expressions. I know if I were a baby, I definitely wouldn't want to be where I wasn't wanted, but who knows? Maybe babies aren't that proud. I was a third child, and my mother only wanted two, but she didn't know how to use her diaphragm. Life is pure gravy to me, and I'm just grateful to be here.

Ironically it was a baby that restored my faith in God. It was my own six-month-old girl. I was changing her diaper when I had a religious revelation. I looked down into the debris and saw a vision of Nature. It was a little green sprout. And it was growing there. Apparently she had excreted a living weed. It was a miracle, I thought. Or something is terribly wrong, I thought again as I rushed her to the hospital in a blind panic. According to the pediatrician it was neither, only a stray banana seed that had sprouted inside her. She told me this phenomenon is quite common in nature, and that some plants can only propagate after having passed through a bird or animal.

That's when the revelation unfolded in all

its true meaning. I pictured myself as a banana tree parent, trying to start a family of young saplings. You see, banana trees have a strategy. They don't just leave their seeds scattered around on the ground.

No, because something could step on the young sprouts. Or some animal might come by and eat them. So they put the seeds in a fruit, a monkey eats it, it goes through him, the seed sprouts inside, and it hits the forest floor with an organic splat.

Now! There is your baby banana tree, right in its own pile of fertilizer. Nobody is going to step on it. And even a warthog knows better than to eat something growing out of a pile of monkey dung. It's a brilliant strategy for survival and propagation.

It's so brilliant, in fact, that Somebody had to figure it out. Somewhere out there, there must exist a Supreme Intelligence doing the brain work for the vegetable kingdom.

So to me, the hand of Almighty God lies revealed in the lowliest pile of primate manure. Naturally I buttonholed my Baptist minister to bring him the good news. I figured he might want to work some monkey dung into his next sermon. But he was born again and was a little out of touch with his roots. You see, he didn't believe in evolution, and in his case, I don't blame him a bit.

As to whether abortion is an indelible blot on The Big Picture or just the smudge of an erased mistake, I'll leave that for the Artist to judge. I don't know whether you have any rights before you're born. All I know is that being born again doesn't entitle you to twice as many.

One of the most interesting paradoxes of the Decade of the Child is that there are tens of thousands of children whom no one cares for or about, thousands more on the way that no one wants, and thousands of couples who will pay almost any price for a child.

A case like this in 1987 led to the most convoluted custody trial since the days of Solomon. The father's name was William Stern. His wife was infertile. The mother's name was Mary Beth Whitehead. Her husband was unemployed.

Of course, the Sterns could have adopted a child, but we all know most of the babies available for adoption are, well, let's just say they would have clashed with their carpeting. Besides, you know how people will talk: "Hey, Bill, nice-looking kid. She's really got your . . . your . . . last name."

In short, he hired Ms. Whitehead to bear a child for him. Normally a woman who carries a child is called a mother, and if it's the result of a paid transaction she is called something quite different, but if you pay her enough and have a contract, she is called a "surrogate mother." Anyway, she changed her mind and kept the child.

Well, Mr. Stern was grief-stricken. The child was his, he claimed. What about the nine long months of pregnancy he had endured the expenses for? What about the pain of childbirth costs? What about the stretch marks on his wallet? What about his capital gains?

There followed hundreds of hours of testimony and television coverage, reams of print commentary, thousands in attorneys' fees—all on behalf of a man, who, let's face it, masturbated into a cup.

It was easy to forget the mother in all of this because we were dealing with a new concept: the sanctity of the sperm. I guess Ms. Whitehead found out the hard way that you can't have a baby without getting screwed somewhere along the line.

So now we have a new complication in obstetrics, the breach-of-contract birth. But why did the whole country turn against this woman because she couldn't turn motherhood into an out-of-body experience? It's sad. But saddest of all is that our civilization has become so devoid of values that the biggest controversy turned out to be who could sell the story rights for the made-for-TV movie.

David Souter has an opinion about all this, but he's not telling us—yet.

9

The Education
President,

or

"LEARN TO READ IN THE PRIVACY
OF YOUR OWN HOME!
GED—High School Diploma
For Free Brochure, Write—
P.O. Box 3051, Akron, OH."

—MATCHBOOK COVER

WE LIVE in a nation of 25 million illiterates. I
read that in *USA Today*. That's a scary
thought, one out of ten adult Americans
can't even read *USA Today*. What are they
all going to do in life? They can't all write
for it. Maybe they can dictate the editorials.

In Japan, the few illiterate individuals are put to work translating VCR instructions into English. But here opportunities are limited.

I like to read, but I'm not one to push my preferences on others. Rather than campaign fruitlessly against the evils of illiteracy, I got a job writing for television

This spring, I found myself sitting in a restaurant, watching a party of young people celebrating. I soon realized they were members of the New York City high school graduating class of 1990, part of that elite 48 percent of New Yorkers that made it all the way through the system.

They were celebrating their unbounded future by dining at Denny's, a restaurant no doubt chosen for its use of pictures on the menu. As I watched them pointing to their selections and puzzling over the arithmetic in a futile attempt to calculate who owed what for the patty melt, it struck me that far too many will face the future ill equipped to tackle the intricacies of *TV Guide* in this age of cable.

It was just their bad luck to go through school before the "Education President" was elected. But it's all a matter of priorities. If they didn't get much out of our shabby, run-down, underfinanced, old school system, maybe they'll do better in our brand-new billion-dollar prison program.

Either way, I'm sure the Education President is concerned about every illiterate one of them. Not as concerned as he'd be if they had an abortion or burned the flag . . . but he cares.

Actually, he should be ashamed. Probably nothing has done more damage to the education opportunities of more kids in the last ten years than the cocaine that started pouring into the country in unprecedented amounts when George Bush took over as head of the South Florida Task Force on Drug Interdiction.

I'm not blaming the then vice president, don't get me wrong. It was nobody's fault. The contras needed beans, and the money had to come from somewhere. When Congress won't authorize money for basic necessities, the people in the government who care are forced to sell drugs to junior high school students to make ends meet. Sometimes it's Afghani heroin, sometimes it might be Cuban cigars, it just so happened this time it was cocaine. Next time, who knows? It might be Afghani heroin again.

In a way, though, I think it's almost common sense to ask ourselves occasionally, Is this drug pushing really worth it? Sure, it's the right thing to do, but what about the effect on the students' grades? Maybe we could just ship a few extra loads a month and spend it on the kids, since they're the ones who bought a lot of the crack that financed the contras. Think of it as a way of giving them something back for all their support. It's a modest proposal.

You see, in education, as in everything, you get what you pay for, and these kids probably do as well on any competency tests as their teachers, which is a tribute to those teachers, considering they're paid almost as well as the prison guards whose functions they have largely assumed. But let's not feel sorry for our teachers. Money isn't everything. What we don't pay them in cash is more than made up for by the prestige of the position.

The priorities of our school system ensure that a Heisman Trophy candidate can earn a thousand dollars for each dollar taken home by the teacher who tore out his or her hair in a vain attempt to give him the tools to decipher the candidate's NFL contract.

Meanwhile, the Japanese are turning out hordes of math and science experts. The problem in sciences is not with schools, however. The problem is what happens out of school. This ad was culled from the *New York Times:*

"Our research division is seeking candidates with a strong background and interest in protein biochemistry. Specific research areas include: mechanism of action of polypeptide hormones and growth factors, ligand-recepter interactions and protein purification, inhibition and characterization. Ideal candidates will have experience in flow cytometry, SDS gel electrophoresis, High Pressure Liquid Chromatography and basic biochemical techniques. Experience in cell culture and sterile technique preferred, 24K."

$24,000! I should add that this is in Manhattan, where you could make that or more without so much as a command of English or a clean shirt, simply by getting in a taxi and claiming you know how to drive. It cost more to put that ad in the paper, per week, than the salary offered. A kid with any intelligence could read that advertisement in the third grade and know better than to go into science. An ad like that does more to discourage science majors than all the rumors of tough courses. Those athletically gifted scholars on science scholarships should be moved in the direction of professional sports for their own good.

As a result of starvation pay in the sciences, the class of '91 will include over 30,000 new lawyers, who will soon be chasing ambulances and sifting through obstetric files, eager to rob someone at the point of a pen. It's a depressing number and yet barely enough to defend the 150,000 white-collar felons who will graduate along with them. When the Japanese take the lead in the high-tech markets, maybe we can sue them to get it back.

And if that doesn't work, maybe we can just take it from them. These days, high school is as good a place as any to learn to dodge bullets. We've definitely educated the cannon fodder. I know there's a lot of macho, freedom-loving bucks out there who would love nothing better than to go over and kick some butt in Iraq. So long as nobody asks them to name the ocean you have to cross to get there.

But no matter, they've witnessed a couple of pushover victories in Grenada, Libya, and Panama, applauding a napping President, although not loudly enough to wake him up.

Now they're fresh from their victories in the video slaughterhouses, the death rattle of a thousand galaxies ringing in their ears.

With the innate belligerence of youth and a fifth-grade reading level, they put their faith in our superior technology, and they look to the sky for their *Challengers*. As the revolution of rising expectations hurtles toward a rendezvous with the anarchy of illiteracy, frustrations will build and never again will it be enough to just say "go at throttle up."

And that raises the question, Who is going to do something about the decline of American excellence? It won't be the Bush generation. All it cares about is getting a capital-gains tax cut. It won't be my generation. All we care about is how we're going to get our Social Security when we retire.

And so I would like to address the coming generation. It's up to you, my sweet young children, to solve the problems your elders have left. No one is going to help you, my friends.

You are indeed the hope of our future. That's why we have invested so much time in thinking about your future. We would have invested money as well, but we're saving that for our own future.

If you are going to be able to support us in the style to which we're accustomed, you're going to have to be healthy, long-lived, hard-working, and clearheaded. That's why I'm calling for a nationwide crack boycott in every high school and junior high in this great land. Don't do it, don't buy it, don't even sell it. As for you elementary school kids, you can help too, by not acting as lookouts. You can do it—for yourselves, and for us, your future dependents. Oh, and by the way, save your money. You'll need it.

10

Busting Butt on Capitol Hill

BEING FED UP with Congress is as universal an emotion as wanting to punch a street mime.

Bush started right out making friends in Congress by not vetoing a $12,000 pay raise for all top federal officials. Congress didn't actually vote to give it to themselves; that would have been unseemly. But its members did vote not to prevent it from automatically happening after voting earlier for a future raise if they didn't vote to prevent it. I should mention that Congress also raised the minimum wage by twenty-five cents an hour, which shows that it cares about those ordinary lower-class working stiffs as well.

Our representatives don't exactly have the easiest job in the world, and they're not likely to get it, either, as long as I'm delivering the commentary on "Weekend Update."

They're busting butt up there on Capitol Hill, and there's no question a pay raise was long overdue. After all, it's not easy trying to raise a family and still put a little something aside for a legal defense fund. Ninety thousand a year doesn't go very far when you're looking at multiple indictments.

My question is, Why can't they get a raise from the military contractors and tobacco lobbyists the way they've always done? I don't dispute that federal salaries are not competitive with those of corporate executives in the private sector. But what better way to keep the corporate sleaze-bags out of government? If salaries are just low enough to keep Lee Iacocca from running for office, that's fine with me.

Of course, the argument is that higher salaries are going to attract more highly qualified people. But if raw ambition and lust for power haven't drawn them in, I don't see where greed is going to be the decisive factor.

If it were, you could just throw your wallet down on the sidewalk and the first one to get to it, make him the President. We could save millions in campaign costs. But say higher salaries do attract better politicians. Say that all over the country honest, far-sighted men of integrity are sitting up and saying, "Another grand a month? Put me on the ballot."

I don't think we want people leaving productive, necessary jobs to go to work for the government. Suppose the Wright brothers had been congressmen? Instead of airplanes, we'd have been fighting the Nazis with kites that cost $10 million apiece.

If we want better people, maybe we should lower the salaries. It seems to work for the teaching profession. When I put this into The Big Picture I can only conclude that now that congressmen are on C-SPAN all the time, they think they're entitled to make as much as Vanna White.

Actually, watching C-SPAN I am constantly humbled by the energy, commitment, and just plain eloquence I see from the floor of both houses and in the committee chambers. Some members are extremely dedicated. Some are brilliant. Not all. Some are embarrassing. But it's all relative. Just because a senator is an ignorant, pretentious fathead doesn't mean he's not a cut above the people who voted for him.

Greed or incompetence on the part of our elected officials is not keeping America from her rightful place of leadership. These constant ethics "scandals" are really getting tedious. Personally, I don't care if a guy gets rich in Congress. If he does one tiny part of what he could do in this time and place in history to make the world more just, and more responsible, or even just more truthful, he should get rich. People get rich for doing something as silly as singing songs or making surgical alterations on perfectly functional noses.

Lyndon Johnson couldn't have stolen enough in his entire lifetime to be adequately compensated for what the Civil Rights Act was worth to this country, let alone the Water Quality Act, Voting Rights Act, Highway Beautification Act, pick one. Pick a dozen.

In any case, we get who we elect. The citizenry has no right to ask a person to be greater in office than he was when he was campaigning, running around kissing everyone's butt, begging money, speaking ill of an opponent he probably didn't even know. Members of the House have to do that every two years! Rain or shine.

Just once, I would like to hear some congressman tell a constituent to quit whining. "Oh, so you're a taxpayer? Wow, I'm impressed. Don't tell me, you're also a member of . . . let me guess . . . the, uh, public? I am honored, sir. You know, it just hit me that since I am a public servant and you are a member of the public that must mean that *I* am *your* servant. Well, let me get you some coffee. Oooops, I spilled it all over you. Sorry, *Master*. Here, let me wipe it off . . . *with my foot."* Then he kicks the petitioner senseless, has him put under arrest, and swaggers out onto the floor to vote himself a pay raise.

The Declaration of Independence notes that King George dissolved the representative houses of the colonies and then adds an interesting concept: "the legislative powers, incapable of annihilation, have returned to the people at large for their exercise." The power to make laws cannot be destroyed.

Sometimes I think the best way to deal with government is to eliminate the candidates altogether. In California, the public can vote directly for the laws, due to a system known as the initiative process. So far, the public has voted to cut state taxes, cut property taxes, cut insurance premiums, and start a lottery. This proves that the citizenry can fool themselves just as well as they can be fooled by a professional politician.

If initiatives catch on, though, I'm going to miss the work of the pros. The Bible says, "The truth shall make you free." But let's not forget it was Spiro Agnew who said that a good lie will keep you out of jail in the first place.

□   104   □

11

Up to Our Ears in Debt

Everybody knows about the deficit—that is, the amount of money Congress spends that it doesn't get from taxes. At first, it sounds great. Most people would say, Let them buy everything with that money and leave me alone. But here is the big problem: They have to borrow the money. Still, most people would say, all the better, I never signed any of those IOUs, and, better yet, I never loaned them anything.

Think of it this way, though: Who has enough money to be loaning it out by the billion to fools like Congress? Only really rich people, like the Japanese and bankers, insurance companies, Germans, and coke dealers. If it was up to me, I'd be happy to let the above groups pay the cost of running the government, but there is a catch.

In order to keep borrowing the money, the U.S. Treasury has to keep paying interest on those T-bills. It pays this interest out of tax money because that's the only cash it has. Right now about one third of all the money you pay in taxes goes to pay that interest. Right off the top. So even if we never pay those idiots back, a great part of our weekly checks go right to the people with most of the money. It's a massive transfer of funds from the poor and middle class straight to the richest of the rich, one of the biggest rip-offs in history.

Every year the deficit is about $200 billion. That doesn't sound like much, I know, but the Treasury doesn't count the interest we're going to have to pay, so actually it's more like $500 billion we go in the hole every year.

The comforting thing is that by comparison it makes the Savings and Loan debt seem a little smaller because it's also about $500 billion. By now I think we are $3 trillion and a half in debt. Somebody should stop and figure out if there even is that much money in the world.

This is not to mention Social Security. The reason, we all know, that we have to pay so much FICA tax right now is so we can save it for when the baby boomers retire, when there will be fewer people working. So we pay the tax, and Social Security invests it for us. But where do they invest it? In the stock market, where we could be making a nice profit? In Japanese companies? No, they loan it to the Treasury, which tosses it into the pot with general funds. In other words, it's being used the same as regular tax money, thereby disguising the size of the deficit even further. Now I don't mind if the Japanese want to loan money to Congress, but it's not wise for the American people to take such a risk with their own money

The Savings and Loan debt is not a pretty debt either. Most of that is owed to the kind of people who sold condos for five times what they paid for them in the early eighties. This came about because at one time S&Ls were only allowed to loan money to people for mortgages. Now that's a pretty good risk because the house is there and you can always take it back if the guy can't make his payments. But Reagan decided these

S&Ls should be able to loan money to anybody with a dream and a flashy tie.

Worm farms, chinchilla ranches, hubcap museums: all of these would have been good investments compared to some of the things the S&Ls funded. They even loaned money to other countries, like Mexico, which shows you how wild they got, since they had never given loans to Mexicans in this country.

It didn't all go to waste, however. At least twenty-nine of the failed Savings and Loans whose debts we are now paying off made extensive loans to companies like Ransom Aviation and Global Air, which were CIA front companies used to siphon funds to the needy in the Nicaraguan highlands. I'm not sure what the money was for, but I think it was something to do with mortgages for contra summer homes in Honduras.

In addition to directly loaning money to the contra cause, which was guaranteed if for some reason they were never paid back, like, say, the contras lost, the S&Ls were able to help out in other ways. They would loan someone the money to buy a building worth a hundred thousand dollars for, say, a million bucks, which seems like a bad deal, but then, a week later, that someone would actually sell it to some swarthy gentleman, for say, ten million, thereby laundering nine million dollars of coke money that could then be donated to some worthy cause. Most likely the million is still owed, I'm sorry to say.

The contras were never a good investment. How much can you trust people who ask for foreign aid when they don't even have a country? Oh, sure, they hoped to get one someday, but don't we all. Where's the collateral? For all we know they just blew the whole wad on Julio Iglesias albums. It would have made just about as much difference in the long run.

Let's step back for a moment and put all this into The Big Picture. There were only 4,000 of these contras, and they were getting at least $100 million a year. That adds up to $25,000 a contra. It's a lot of velvet paintings, my friends.

With the same amount of money we could have sent them all to Harvard Law School. By now they would be lawyers, and they would be suing the entrenched Sandinista bureaucracy for one thing or another, happily living on the backs of the proletariat.

As for the plight of the Nicaraguan people themselves, what can I say? It's a tough world. Of course, they're used to being oppressed. After all, they're Catholics.

*   *   *

There are many paranoid conspiracy theories about who runs the economy: the multinationals, the oil companies, the Jews, the Rosicrucians, the Pope, the Mafia. But none of them is as scary as the truth: No one's in charge. It's every man for himself. The economy is nothing more than the human version of the food chain.

Any conclusion about the economy can be reached by examination of data. As an example let's make our own analysis, putting the symptoms into The Big Picture: Imports are up, productivity is down; we're in debt up to our ears, and our banks are reeling under a load of ill-considered loans to Latin America. The answer is obvious: The problem is pot.

What else comes from a foreign country, makes you show up late for work, spend more than you earn, and loan money to Mexicans? Before we slap quotas on the Japanese for making cars as if their jobs depended on it, we should check our trade deficit with Colombia. It won't be easy, because it's all in small bills. But it's in the billions. And it's no wonder, because in the real world people are never going to "just say no" to something that's a proven cure for PMS. Just as a gift item alone it's going to be a substantial addition to our trade deficit.

Which naturally brings up the other broken nose in our financial profile, the farm crisis. American consumers are being forced to import an agricultural substance that our own farmers can grow better than anyone else in the world. And yet the one thing on which all economists agree is that a fool and his money are as easily parted by a guy named Dave as they are by a guy named Paco.

In other words, our only real choice is whether we want those recreational greenbacks going to prop up some puppet in Panama or to finance some ex-hippie's solar-heated hot tub in Humboldt County. In addition, consider this: If American farmers could grow pot, we could sell it to the Japanese. Then the quality of their merchandise would go down to match ours.

The seeds of competitiveness are stored in plastic film cans all over this great nation. Let's bring them out from under those Gro-Lites and into the sunshine, where they can do our trading partners some serious damage.

In understanding our economy, the important thing is to first understand what a trade deficit is. Basically, it's when you buy something more from somebody than you sell to them. The reason I know this is because I personally ran a trade deficit with a guy named Jorge in the early seventies. And it's bad. I mean, on the one hand, it was only money—a few bucks I saved on my taxes. But, it's American greenbacks. And that means that Jorge, an illiterate, semipsychotic parasite from the barrios of Bogotá is now entitled to a hard day's work from some upstanding, honest American laborer because he's holding the U. S. dollars. This is an evil of capital outflow.

The trade deficit affects all Americans, whether a Japanese banker is buying your office building or a Haitian immigrant is taking your job at the gas station. Most of it is caused by the Japanese because they don't play fair—I heard a congressman say this and I know he was giving me the straight stuff because he was running for President at the time. The reason they don't play fair is that they are selling us things cheaper then we can make them ourselves. This is bad enough, but sometimes they even sell us things cheaper then *they* can make them.

This is called dumping—selling below cost—and it's considered a serious rip-off. Now, when someone can actually rip you off by selling to you below cost, that's shrewd. There's no way you can compete with someone who can do that. Now if Jorge were to try that he would be fairly popular, until he went broke. But the Japanese do it, and no one likes them.

And the thing is, even when we bust these burn artists for dumping, they can still rip us off by making us overcharge them for our merchandise! That's how slick they are. They do it with things called tariffs, duties, and import fees. We have these things in America, too, but only for products made by companies that have an ex-Cabinet member on the board of directors.

I've heard a lot of talk about the need to "level the playing field" and break down foreign trade barriers. We all know the Japanese would gladly trade in their Hondas and the Germans their BMWs if only they could somehow get their hands on a Chevette.

I doubt we will ever make things well enough to sell to the Japanese, and probably we shouldn't try. We never sold a lot of things to Japan anyway, as far as I remember. The solution is for us to start making things well enough for *ourselves* to buy. If Ford and GM could just crack the American market they wouldn't have to worry about the Japanese.

But, that's why the opening of Eastern Europe is so exciting because we already make plenty of things well enough to sell there. The Polish market might be just the thing to get Chrysler back on its feet. How hard can it be? The East Germans have a car, the Trabant, that they used not to be able to trade at the border for a pair of Nikes. We can't afford to let Trabant get in there ahead of us.

This also makes the Latin American debt a serious priority because, once again, we do make things well enough to sell to them, provided we loan them the money first. Which we can't do right now because they already owe us so much they can't even pay the interest.

How we got into this mess is more than interesting. (Well, it's different from interesting, anyway.) First, we had all the money in the world, and then we could loan the rest of the world all the money they needed to buy things from us. But then, suddenly, the Arabs got a bunch of the money by raising the price of oil. So we raised the price of everything else to try and get it back, thereby forcing the Arabs to put their money in the bank like everyone else.

Our banks then loaned the money to Third World countries with undeveloped oil resources, like Mexico, figuring they could drill for oil and pay it back. So, they drilled for oil, and they found it, and the price collapsed, and they couldn't pay it back.

So where is all that money now? Well, I forgot to mention that many underdeveloped countries have to borrow money for their politicians to steal since they don't have enough lobbyists to support them in any kind of decent style. Also, their elections arc rigged, which makes it hard to justify taking campaign contributions under the table. In any case, to make a long story short, most of the money is back in a bank in Miami under the name Gonzalez.

The problem is very complex, as is any problem involving international finance. I have a solution, but I hesitate to reveal the details here, not wishing to embarrass the upcoming Group of Seven meeting with its graceful simplicity. Suffice to say it involves ten pesos and a chain letter.

PART THREE

The World
and
The Big Picture

12

The Environment, or The Tale of an Old Tar

THE WILD SEAS crashed around him, filling his soul with their beauty and rage. He took another pull out of his flask and watched an iceberg float by.

"Come here, son," the captain called to his third mate. "Take the wheel. I'm going downstairs to see demons for a few hours. Don't fall overboard, and try not to hit a state." So began the wreck of the *Exxon Val-*

dez. The effects will linger for years, maybe decades. It seems the only thing we've learned from it all is that Alaskans don't know how to pronounce Spanish.

Exxon claims that it's spent $60 million on the cleanup effort, which sounds like a lot, until you consider that for every dollar they spent cleaning up oil, they spent two more publicizing how much money they spent cleaning up oil.

This was an ecological catastrophe, thousands of square miles of our most pristine wilderness oozing with millions of gallons of crude oil.

Oil company officials assured us that as nature-loving citizens themselves, they were deeply concerned. Exxon spokesmen were everywhere on television—calm, reasonable, the very voice of civic responsibility. By pure luck the firm had plenty of articulate, photogenic vice presidents on hand, having made room for them by firing the entire staff of spill experts three years earlier.

"We folks here at Exxon, as guardians of this great nation's natural resources, accept complete responsibility for this unavoidable spill, for which we are not liable. Like all of you, we are appalled at the waste of precious petroleum. However, we're also proud to announce that most, if not all, of the financial loss can be reversed simply by raising the price of gasoline. We know there are those who will say, 'Well and good, but what about the wildlife?' Well, it's too late for them, and that's a shame. However, in the unlikely event that such a thing should happen again, our research scientists are developing a technique that will enable us to wring out and salvage up to ninety percent of the oil from every bird, fish and sea otter we can recover." I never actually heard the above statement, but I distinctly remember it.

The spill itself was bad enough, but the damage was greatly increased by a complete lack of leadership in the crucial few days immediately following. This is one thing we can't blame on the President, though. For one thing, he just happens to be an environmentalist. I know this because he said so himself during the campaign.

I don't doubt he would have stepped in and taken control of the situation himself if he hadn't been so busy cleaning up Boston Harbor. His comment on the *Valdez* matter was, "Let's not do anything irresponsible to make sure this doesn't happen again." He actually said that.

But it will happen again, that we know. It

happens all the time. Since the *Exxon Valdez* spill there have been about a dozen in New York Harbor. Around there, though, it's kind of hard to tell. The only sure way is to check the beaches. If the syringes washing up have oil in them, there's probably been a spill. One local inlet, the Kill Van Kull, has had so much oil spilled into it that it's been placed in the Strategic Reserve System.

Oil spills could turn out to be one of the least of our worries. Although ozone depletion doesn't mean our sky is falling out, it's definitely thinning on top. Not to mention that the rain forests are falling faster than a fundamentalist preacher's pants in a cheap motel room.

The greenhouse phenomenon means that the earth is getting warmer. But if that is so, then, according to the first law of thermodynamics, space is getting colder as well. It has to be. Of course, it doesn't really affect us, and the cooling is so infinitesimal as to be immeasurable, but still, it's happening.

Indeed, the last few years have been like a nature hike through the Book of Revelation. Earthquakes, famine, drought, pestilence, plague, it's all in the newspapers. Maybe it's not on the color weather map, but it's there.

Species are becoming extinct before we've

even had a chance to exploit them. Now maybe some of these disappearing species have only themselves to blame. It's a documented fact that the passenger pigeon just wasn't working hard enough. Everybody knows the white rhino just plain has a bad attitude.

But when you consider that the snow leopard has come to the brink of extinction while the Pekinese has doubled its population this decade, it's obvious that somebody hasn't thought this thing through.

Yet with all these serious problems, people are actually wasting hundreds of man-hours protesting outside cancer clinics because guinea pigs are being used as guinea pigs. Voices are raised in anguish because white rats are used in medical research. Just because they're white doesn't give them any special status as far as I'm concerned. Rats are rats, and for all the disease and plague they caused in the Middle Ages, they owe us.

Saint George killed the last dragon, and he was called a hero for it. I've never even seen a dragon, and I wish he would have left at least one. Saint Patrick made a name for himself by running the snakes out of Ireland, leaving the place vulnerable to rodent infestation. This business of making saints out of men who exterminate their fellow creatures has got to stop. All I'm saying is, it's starting to get a little lonely up here at the top of the food chain.

I thought I could do my own small part to save the planet by becoming a vegetarian. Actually, I did it not so much because I love animals but because I hate plants. I still like to hunt, though. In fact, I've found that plants are a lot easier than animals to sneak up on.

I cut down my own Christmas tree every year, but I stalk it for a few hours first. I bagged a seventy-eight pointer last season. I surprised him in a clearing. He was just standing there, growing, and throwing off oxygen like there was no tomorrow, dreaming his evergreen dreams. Oh, he was cunning. He thought he'd be safe there in front of the courthouse.

But when I got him home, he was still alive. I should have put him out of his misery, but 'twas the season to be jolly. So I put him in water to make sure he didn't die too quickly. Then I drilled thumbscrews into his little trunk and dressed him up with humiliating balls and stringed tin junk.

The whole family piled presents at his feet, and, just for a tease, we led him to believe they were his. While the rest of us celebrated the coming of the Prince of Peace in the spirit of goodwill to all mankind, he withered and died in my living room.

At last he surrendered his essence into the air he helped create, leaving the sweet scent of his corpse as one last gift to the lumbering race. Finally, I ditched him in my neighbor's yard.

Although we have an extinction rate unmatched since the Mesozoic era, extinction is only one among many of our environmental tragedies. The most tragic, perhaps, but not the most visible.

Next to the *Exxon Valdez* spill, the biggest environmental mess I've personally witnessed was Central Park the morning after Earth Day. I don't know who first came up with the idea that we could save the planet by swilling beer and listening to a free concert, but it certainly has caught on.

In some areas Earth Day is celebrated by planting trees. Of course, they are all cut down again at Christmas, but it's the thought that counts. In fact, it is thought that is the solution.

Because in The Big Picture, the first cause of environmental degradation is ignorance, and especially illiteracy. Vast numbers of people who can't read give us directions at service stations, causing the waste of millions of gallons of gasoline.

Thousands more foolishly defrost their refrigerators with sharp objects, thereby releasing chlorofluorocarbons into the atmosphere. It's all the more reason to plant trees, because they give us two of the most crucial elements for our survival—oxygen and books.

13

The End of the Nuclear Age

I HAVE always thought the nuclear threat was blown way out of proportion. I have a feeling our descendants are going to look back at all this nuclear hysteria from the bottom of their toxic-waste dumps and laugh their feelers off. Philosophically, I would much rather die in a nuclear holocaust along with three or four hundred million of my fellow world citizens than die alone in the gutter from some chemical-induced cancer. I suppose that's because I'm basically a people person.

The biggest danger from a nuclear device is not getting hit by one, but living near a place where they make them. In Rocky Flats, near Denver, the nuke makers are missing enough plutonium to make seven bombs. They actually *lost* forty pounds of plutonium. They think it might be in the air ducts somewhere—or maybe behind the couch. No one is really sure.

Some of the places where we made and tested our nuclear weapons are so contaminated they might as well have been hit by one. Even if they can be cleaned up, there is no place to dump the stuff. The nukers can sweep it up, but they can't empty the dustpan. Now that the magnitude of the problem is emerging, the Defense Department says the only just and fair solution may be to do what they should have done a long time ago: give the land back to the Indians.

Timing is everything in The Big Picture. The Indians fought the paleface for almost 250 years, and when you think about it, they lost just in time. Weaponry has changed incredibly fast. It's amazing to think that Hiroshima was only sixty-nine years after Little Big Horn. If the Sioux had just held on half as long as they'd been fighting already, they would now be up against the General Dynamics "Tomahawk"-cruise missile.

*　　*　　*

How would you explain such a weapon to Sitting Bull? Put it into The Big Picture and you have a spear fletched with feathers of fire that flies over the mountains at four times the speed of sound from the other side of the world, following the contours of the terrain a hundred feet above the ground. It has a map of the continent in three dimensions on a flake of crystal no bigger than a thumbnail, and the trail to the target is woven into its nose with threads of lightning.

It comes with a noise that flattens the trees and stretches the ground like the head of a drum and a wind that snaps off green grass at the roots. It makes a light brighter than a thousand suns and turns the earth to molten glass for five miles in every direction, and no people can live there for a hundred thousand years. That is, if it works the way the defense contractors promise. Sometimes it looks as if we may never find out. How convenient for General Dynamics.

Harry Truman is still the only man to ever use one of those spears on living people. He had his moods. It was a decision he made himself. In fact, he didn't even tell the country until it was over. The next day on the radio he said, "The force from which the sun draws its power has been loosed against those who brought war to the Far East."

He was a brave warrior, Harry, and he never looked back. He bore that burden alone and he left his country with no nuclear blood on its hands. He's still paying the price, too, because, to this day, Truman's birthplace in Independence, Missouri, is the only tourist attraction in America where you never see Japanese with cameras.

The only chance any of us might have to see nuclear explosions would be at Muroroa Atoll, where the French occasionally test their warheads. As you can imagine, New Zealand, which is downwind, objects to this because it keeps them up late at night and interferes with their TV reception. Plus, according to New Zealand, the South Pacific isn't zoned for nuclear testing.

The French have a different point of view. They say that if they are going to have nuclear weapons, they need to test them, to make sure they're safe. I mean, the last thing you want in the middle of a nuclear holocaust is some kind of accident.

Personally, I have a feeling these nuclear tests are just a cover for France to fish over the limit, which is always a temptation when you have a boatload of warheads and plenty of time on your hands. A couple of kilotons over the side and it's raining mackerel for days.

Greenpeace, the environmental TAC squad, got involved in this dispute at one point, begging France to give it a rest. The French just laughed, but the attention of the entire world began to focus on French nuclear policy. Greenpeace then had the gall to place itself in the danger zone in an attempt to stop the tests.

The delicate diplomacy for which the French are historically renowned is generally reserved for dealing with nations stronger than themselves. New Zealand doesn't qualify. Somebody blew up the Greenpeace ship as it lay at harbor. Worldwide, outrage over the Muroroa incident recruited thousands into the nuclear-freeze movement, which went the way of all enterprises motivated by good intentions. The beginning of the end of the nuclear age didn't come until Chernobyl, and it's on a solid foundation, motivated by raw fear.

And so it is that the most important event of the Reagan administration was a mistake. While that in itself is far from ironic, it is ironic that it wasn't one of his.

The Chernobyl meltdown gave the world a taste of nuclear reality.

At the time, it was no big disaster by Soviet standards. According to the government, only two people were killed. That's nothing compared to the eleven people who died in the Stalinist purges. Not to mention the 269 CIA spies who blew themselves up in that Korean airliner. But like all their other problems, the numbers kept getting bigger with *glasnost.*

In defense of the Soviets, I think we can all relate to keeping silent after blowing out a colossal cloud of noxious gas among friends—but if it's radioactive, you have a duty to own up. You sure can't blame it on the dog.

The first benefactor of Chernobyl was the INF Treaty. Intermediate nuclear forces have a range of 500 to 3,000 miles. A weapon like that must give you a dubious feeling of security, like having a cobra on a six-inch leash.

After Chernobyl the nuclear strategy of both the U.S. and the U.S.S.R. shifted to favor longer-range weapons. The longer the better. If you can aim at your enemy, it's too close to nuke him. And if you have the wind in your face, anywhere in the hemisphere is too close.

The aftereffects of the accident were so

widespread and long-lasting that the doctrine of mutually assured destruction lost its credibility. When INF negotiations started, they had the sincere blessing for the first time of battlefield commanders, and an entire class of nuclear weapons was eliminated, as the administration has boasted so many times. It could as easily boast that it was only 2 percent of all nuclear warheads, something like taking one BB out of a fully loaded Daisy.

So, we got the treaty, and the Great White Father in Washington can file it with all the other treaties ready for the time when a bright new generation of glory-crazed physics geeks gloms enough grant money to make it all moot.

But let us never forget that the credit for that treaty should go neither to Reagan nor Gorbachev, but to the unnamed Ukrainian, probably alcoholic, who forgot to turn the valve back on at Reactor #2. May God rest his soul and his family not have to pay for the bullets. Let him be remembered for something, for he belongs to history.

PART FOUR

The Peoples of the World and The Big Picture

14

Races vs. Races

"A people without history is like the wind on the buffalo grass."

—SIOUX SAYING

THE HISTORY of America begins with the Indians. I'm part Indian, and so are a lot of Americans who don't know it. Indian blood was not something our grandparents liked to brag about. They liked to pass themselves off as all white if they could get away with it (because they couldn't buy drinks, for one thing).

My ancestors were a particularly homely tribe of dried-fish eaters in northern Michigan, the Ottawas. They were shrewd and thrifty, with large, sagging earlobes and a tendency toward baldness. They dug copper out of the hills above Lake Superior and traded it as far as what is now Guatemala.

Two hundred years before the Revolution, a canoe appeared from the east, paddled by white, hairy men with bad teeth and stinking feet. They were French, with nifty things to trade for beaver pelts, and gradually their genes improved the tribal looks.[*]

By the time the Ottawa homeland became part of the Union in 1837, the Indians were almost presentable. Just about then a lot of people carrying axes showed up in the woods, and shade began to get a little scarce.

My ancestors gave names to all the rivers and lakes, the cities, towns, and counties, and the state. Then they laid their language in a grave beside their spoken history, scattered their arrowheads in fields so boys could find them in the years to come, and disappeared into history.

Other tribes went down fighting, but it was all the same. On the one hundredth anniversary of the republic, in 1876, sometime around the Fourth of July, Indians won their last victory, at Little Big Horn.

Nobody knows just what day it was be-

[*] The English settlers claimed it was the other way around.

cause the Indians didn't name the days of the week. They measured time by important events that occurred. They called that particular day "The Day We Killed Custer."

Later, they were exterminated as a race. Still, the Indians who knew Custer say it was worth it just to have put Yellowhair in his place, he was such a pompous ass.

You have to admit Custer was one of the biggest idiots in American history. A glory-crazed army lifer rushing off to make a big dramatic last stand against a race about five years away from complete extinction anyway. He could have checked into a hotel and waited.

My ancestors were generally a peaceful people, on both sides. In fact, there is no record of anyone in my family ever having served in the military of any country. I'm basically descended from a long line of cowards. I'm not necessarily proud of that. On the other hand, there are a lot of Browns in the world today. If you don't believe me, just look us up in the phone book. Then as a comparison, see if you can find a Custer.

I never thought much about my Indian heritage until I was eight or nine and we took that trip to Lookout Mountain, Tennessee. Remember the Indian souvenir stand, where

I bought that hand-crafted toy tomtom that had "Made in Japan" on the bottom? At first I assumed there were Indians in Japan, thereby reversing the colossal case of mistaken identity that caused Columbus to give the Indians their name.

My father was only too happy to inform me that I had been cheated by an island full of devious little yellow savages whose asses we had kicked in the last war because they were too primitive to understand American technology. They also made party favors and stocking stuffers, he told me.

In retrospect, I think it's ironic that when the Japanese decided to penetrate the American market, and I use that in the fullest sense of the word, the first people they put out of business were the Indians.

It seems like every time a new race targets the American continent, the Indians have a bad day. That's their luck. First somebody comes over the Atlantic and takes their land, and then somebody comes over the Pacific and takes their souvenir business.

I picture that poor Cherokee on Lookout Mountain, living in a refugee camp in his own country, water-skiers roaring up and down his favorite fishing holes, teenage girls in pedal pushers having picnics all over his hunting grounds. His Studebaker's been up on blocks all summer, his dog has worms, and every time he turns on the TV one of his relatives is getting shot off a horse.

So he sits down to knock out a few of the primitive handicrafts his grandmother taught him how to make the week she was sober, hoping to pick up a few bucks off the paleface tourists. Meanwhile, halfway around the world, an emerging industrial giant has just targeted the beaded belt and rubber tomahawk market as the beachhead of their economic invasion of the United States.

They say history repeats itself, and the proof of it is they've said it before. But who knows? Two hundred years from now, maybe the Japanese will tell their schoolchildren how they bought Manhattan for a paltry few billion dollars' worth of electronic trinkets. That may be the price of the American Dream.

Under the Statue of Liberty there's a plaque that carries a poem by Emma Lazarus that says:

> Give me your tired, your poor,
> Your huddled masses yearning to breathe
>   free,
> The wretched refuse of your teeming
>   shore.

Send these, the homeless, tempest-tossed,
  to me:
I lift my lamp beside the golden door.

Well, I think it's about time to stop all this name-calling.

The American Dream has been an elusive dream for some among us. I guess one of the best examples comes from the annals of rock and roll history. It's a story about a man who came to be called "The King" in a democracy. He was a poor kid who grew up in Tupelo, Mississippi, and came of age in the early fifties. All he had was a guitar, a flashy shirt, and a wiggle in his hip. But he also had that certain something called talent. Unfortunately, he was black, and he never made a nickel with his music. But two years later Elvis Presley came along and made a fortune doing exactly the same thing.

We've made a lot of progress toward a more just society. When I was a kid, I remember segregated drinking fountains. We don't have those anymore. In fact, we don't have any drinking fountains that work anymore. So progress always comes at a price.

The greatest change has been in the South. A couple of years ago, there was an ugly racial incident in Forsyth County, Georgia. I remember the headline: "Bigots Found in Georgia." I guess it was a slow news day.

It's all too easy for Northerners to think of blatant bigotry as the province of an entrenched white-trash subclass in the rural South. But I ask you, is it really fair to blame all white trash for the actions of those few? Just because a man has a few engine blocks in his front yard, drinks cheap liquor out of a jelly jar, and sleeps with his sister now and then—that doesn't make him a bigot. I speak for a lot of white trash when I say we resent being lumped in with the redneck peckerwoods.

The South is rising again. For most of the past decade, it's boomed. Part of the reason is air conditioning. The population explosion in the Sunbelt almost exactly coincides with the introduction of central cooling as a standard feature in new buildings. But the main reason is the increased participation of blacks in a reorganized society.

Martin Luther King predicted that the economic salvation of the South would be the legal salvation of its black population. He was right. You can't keep a man in the gutter unless you get down there yourself and hold him.

Strangely, the exact opposite has happened in some cities of the North. When I first visited Mississippi as a child, it was like a Third World country. The same could now be said about Detroit, and the reason is the same: racial discrimination. A white in Detroit feels the same fear as a black in Alabama in the fifties. There is a virtual curfew on the streets; a white person out after dark is fair game. The mayor, Coleman Young, has about as much use for whites as Bull Connor had for blacks. This is not reverse racism because there is no such thing. It's racism.

It's worth defining the word racism in light of the racial incidents lately in New York City.

The first of the recent racial incidents to make the front page of the *New York Post* was Howard Beach. Three black men were assaulted by a gang of whites just because they were in a white neighborhood at night. One of them was struck by a car and killed trying to escape. That's racism. For some reason people expect white neighborhoods to be safer. It turns out they are, but mainly for white people. In the Bensonhurst section of Brooklyn a young black man was killed by a bunch of white hoodlums. Again, racism. During the trial of one of his killers, the attorney for the accused was attacked outside the courtroom by a mob of angry blacks. This was not racism, however. It was confusion. He should have been attacked because he was a lawyer.

A young black woman named Tawana Brawley was found in a plastic bag in a vacant lot, alive, but smeared with dog feces and racial epithets. She claimed she had been raped and held hostage by five white cops. Mike Tyson gave her a watch. Bill Cosby offered her a scholarship. It later turned out to have all been a hoax.

Her story was full of holes from the beginning, but no one dared call her a liar for fear of being branded a racist. There were a number of people who wanted it to be true, and most of them were black.

Recently she showed up at a trial in support of three black teenagers accused in the brutal gang rape of a white woman who had been jogging in Central Park. Two of them confessed on videotape, blandly describing how they beat her and left her for dead. They didn't rape her, though, they only held her while the others did. Obviously, they expected lenient treatment for this consideration. Tawana Brawley was there, believe it or not, to show support for the accused. This is not considered racism, but a necessary part of "the movement." A movement it is, one way or the other.

In San Francisco, concern for black sensitivity has reached the point where newspapers don't even mention the race of a criminal. A local paper recently printed the description of a rapist who was still at large, height, weight, age, but not his race. Actually, this is racism because the implication is that it's understood.

Jimmy the Greek was forced into retirement for saying blacks had large thighs. Here's a man who for years got away with calling himself "The" Greek, as if there were no others. He wiped out 2,000 years of Hellenic credibility with a mere twelve years of bad picks. And yet never a complaint from another Greek. Blacks should be so forbearing.

In another incident, Actors' Equity, the actors' union, recently denied sanction for a British actor to play a Eurasian character on Broadway because it said the part should go to an Asian. (They later relented.) What made their decision so ridiculous was that the character is half French, half Vietnamese. If the show played in Asia, would the Asian actors' union deny the part to someone because he wasn't European? This is racism, because Equity's unspoken assumption is that if you have any nonwhite ancestors at all, you're nonwhite.

Recently a gang of black teenagers attacked a group of Vietnamese because they thought they were Koreans. Now the Koreans are offended at the idea that they look like Vietnamese. It's all relative, but as you can see racial tension has been high in the Big Apple, America's microcosm.

I know it's not easy being black in New York City for numerous reasons. Taxis won't stop for you. Every crackhead panhandler on the street thinks he has the right to call you brother. On top of all that, you have to open the paper in the morning and read that Al Sharpton has just appointed himself your spokesman.

Yes, it's tough being a minority in New York, but that's not racism, that's just New York. It's tough being a kid here, too, and it's tough being old. It's tough being a woman, and it's tough being gay. There are 6 million minorities in the Naked City, and we all belong to at least one of them. Just because somebody hates you doesn't give you any special privileges. There have been a lot of innocent people murdered there this year, and there will be next year, and the year after that. They will be black, white, yellow, brown, and occasionally even an unlucky red man. We can't change that. All we can do is try to ensure that those people are killed for their money or their driving habits, not for the color of their skins. The end of bigotry will come not when all minorities are judged by the same standard, but when all bigots are.

The song says about New York, if you can make it there, you can make it anywhere. Well, that's not quite true. Ask any Haitian, or Nigerian, or Vietnamese, or Honduran, or Russian Jew, or Palestinian, or Pakistani. They're making it here, and they couldn't make it there. Because it's a free country. If you can't make it here, you can't make it anywhere.

The racial barriers are indeed down—not completely, but enough to jump over with a little effort. That scares some people, because discrimination is a good excuse not to try, and if you don't try, you can't fail. The truth is that in America, in 1991, whether you're black or white or Michael Jackson, you are what you make yourself. Let's make ourselves a little less strident.

15

The Wars of the World

It's a cliché to say it's a small planet, but that would never stop me from saying it. In The Big Picture everything is as interrelated as an Appalachian coal town.

If there is a theme to this century, it might be the death of ancient tribalism. The urbanization of the global village. A leveraged buy-out of the cultural assets of humanity, where the farmer's market of national identities merges into a giant worldwide mall. But I do know that everything in The Big Picture exists in time and space, and there-

fore everything has both a history and a geography. The geography of the world is
completely known these days, as is that of
the moon and even Mars. How odd that a
third of our fellow citizens in these times
should know less about their global neighborhood than a contemporary of Columbus.
More people know what sign they are than
on what continent they live.

We spend billions every year making sure
we have geography on our side in any future
war. Right now we're negotiating the rent
on our base at Subic Bay, the Philippines. It
will probably be around a hundred million.
It's worth it, though, just to keep the Solomon Islands defended. We can't have the
world's richest source of guano just lying out
in plain sight in the middle of the Pacific,
completely undefended.

The entire southern flank of the International Date Line would be exposed, dangling
before the Soviets like a sardine at Sea
World. Suppose the Soviets made a surprise
attack, snapped up the Date Line, and
moved it to Moscow? They could launch an
attack the day before yesterday.

To our south, elections in Nicaragua seem to
have put an end to the Sandinista threat,
although the contras haven't disbanded as I

write this. Now they're raising their ugly heads again. The excuse for funding the right in both Nicaragua and El Salvador is the danger of communism spreading to Mexico. I say don't worry about it. I mean really, what possible appeal could Marxism have for the starving, illiterate, debt-ridden, hopeless peasants of Mexico?

Now you take these rebels in El Salvador. They work for nothing. That's because they're Communists, and they don't know any better. The Salvadoran military, which we fund, charges us a couple of hundred million a year. This proves that our guys are smarter, but it doesn't say much for our own intelligence.

It has been said that war is obsolete now that we have nuclear weapons. This is true in much the same sense that knives and chopping boards are obsolete now that we have Cuisinarts.

Take the case of Iraq. Its war with Iran was the deadliest war of my lifetime. It made our Civil War look like Vietnam. They fought for nine years, and over a million men died. I doubt if any of them ever figured out why. No one else ever did.

As far as most Americans could tell, Iran and Iraq were fighting because their names were too much alike. They were getting each other's mail. Iran wanted Iraq to change its name to "boot-licking lackey of the degenerate she-devil."

Actually, the whole thing started over a property claim over 2,500 years old, which tells us something about the speed of Islamic bureaucracy. It also makes me wonder how the issue ever popped up in conversation after all that time.

It could have been as simple as a guy with a bad attitude talking to his buddies after a beheading in Iraq: "You know, Habib, that Persian land grab back in 500 B.C. is really starting to stick in my craw. Wake up the kids and give them guns, we're going to war."

We never knew who to root for in this war. Most Americans were vindictive enough to have daydreams about the Ayatollah dangling from a lamppost in Baghdad, but only because we didn't know very much about the guy who started it all, Saddam Hussein. Now we know him all too well.

The State Department thought of him as a moderate Arab. A moderate Arab, by the way, is one who holds a grudge for only eight generations. Our first hint that he had higher ambitions came in 1980 when he bought a nuclear reactor from France and launched his own version of the Manhattan Project.

In The Big Picture, giving Iraq a nuclear bomb is like giving a chain saw to a termite. The Israelis had no choice but to take the time out of their busy lunch hour to blow it off the map.

As we've seen, this was only a minor setback for Saddam. With German help, he was able to begin production of poison gas. It is not known why Hussein settled on Germany as his supplier of choice for poison-gas technology. Perhaps it was their solid track record.

Unlike the Germans, though, Saddam never got to use his gas against Jews. He found it worked just as well on Kurds, however. And when he was faced with a morale problem among his soldiers on the Iranian front, poison gas turned out to be just the ticket to deal with 10,000 or so Iraqi deserters hiding out in the marshes around Fao.

As I write this our own soldiers are encamped not 150 miles from those marshes. Contrary to the carping of isolationist cynics (rare as it is), our boys are not there to die for cheap oil. That, you can be sure, is not reason enough to challenge a man who once boasted that "America is not a society that can stand to lose ten thousand men in a single battle."

Our volunteer army is arrayed against the Iraqi martyrs for a lofty principle of international law: that no country shall invade another—unless, of course, the leader of that country is suspected of drug dealing. We stand in the desert sand to protect the fundamental rights of all nations not to be occupied by force, unless the nation doing the occupying is absolutely certain it needs the occupied territory for reasons of security or as a place to settle recent immigrants.

We stand for this principle not alone, but with our good friend and ally Hafaz al-Assad of Syria, a well-known protector of such laws. I understand Idi Amin is coming to our side, too, as soon as he takes off a few pounds.

I saw Saddam Hussein on CNN, giving his side of the story. He reminded me of the Reverend Gene Scott, but Gene Scott is a touch more succinct. I'd just like to clear one thing up—his claim that Kuwait is historically part of Iraq because they were both part of the Ottoman Empire. That's ridiculous. Just because two dogs get kicked by the same guy doesn't make them a litter. This goes to show how evil and ruthless Saddam

Hussein is—using historical arguments on American television viewers. He will exploit any weakness.

It's not going to be easy to de-Saddamize Kuwait, and thank God we don't have to do it by ourselves. We have 4,000 French troops behind us, not to mention several from the Benelux countries. And, of course, if we get in real trouble there are reinforcements from Bangladesh. I wonder what their K rations look like. Somehow I just can't see a Bengladeshi soldier complaining about the food. Let's not forget the Egyptian contingent, either. I know it's important to have them on our side, but really, when was the last time Egypt won a war? They may have beaten the Nubians in 1504 B.C. But that was almost 3,500 years ago. People say the Red Sox fans have patience.

The President has given his word that Kuwait will be liberated, and now our troops will have to back it up. It's fine for a President to make promises he doesn't keep *before* he's elected. We expect that. But when he makes them after he's elected, it becomes a matter of national honor. Saddam will not keep Kuwait, believe that.

As to the "new world order" we all keep hearing about, we're going to need it as long as our energy policy can be summed up in four words—"send in the troops."

If there is anything good that comes from this, it is the end of Arab daydreaming about an Arab nation. Perhaps they'll find that the reality they have been desperately ignoring for three decades is easier to face than Iraqi tanks. Israel is not going away, and neither are the people who used to live there, the Palestinians. It's about time the Arabs and the Jews grew up a little.

These people have been fighting for 5,000 years and they can't even agree on what year it is. They have more in common than they are willing to admit. In fact, if it weren't for the fact that the Israelis are always morally right I would have a hard time telling them apart. On the other hand, aren't the Arabs always morally right, too?

The Jews of Palestine live in a tough part of the world, surrounded by sworn enemies, about as secure as a trailer park in tornado country. But let it be said they've treated the Palestinians under their jurisdiction with the kind of justice and compassion that can be appreciated only by American Indians. The Arab countries treat them no better, which is often used as an argument to excuse Israel. It doesn't.

The Palestinians are powerless, oppressed, burning with resentment over grievances unredressed, pyromaniacs in a petrified forest. It's no wonder they throw rocks. Their houses are bulldozed, their lands appropriated, and if they are caught throwing stones at soldiers, their hands are broken. They're ignored if they speak, beaten if they shout.

It's never been easy to keep the peace in Palestine. In The Big Picture, there will be peace in Israel and the rest of the Middle East. And also in Eastern Europe. Call me a dreamer. The trend does seem to be toward sanity. And after all, we've already seen the fall of Marxism.

16

The End of Communism

How IRONIC that the fatal flaw of communism
would turn out to be that there is no money
in it. It just seems fitting, in a way, considering what communism is. "To each according to his need, from each according to his
ability." It sounds great in a café over ten
cups of expresso, especially if you're really
poor and have no ability.

The Bolsheviks had a good theory. They
figured if you took the financial incentive out
of exploiting the masses, no one would
bother. How were they to know people

would exploit each other just for the fun of it? Under communism, instead of a greedy boss, the worker ends up with a boss who is always in a bad mood because he's broke.

The entire Communist world is in a state of decay. They're beating us in space satellites, but they've never been to the moon. They have the Bolshoi, but no MTV. They can dance, but they can't moon-walk. People are leaving in droves, there is rampant corruption, ethnic strife, a disintegrating infrastructure and a collapsing industrial base. The Soviet bureaucracy is about as efficient as a Mexican traffic court that doesn't take bribes. All they need is crack and Russia would be as bad as the Bronx.

To us the Russians seem like paranoid, uptight honkies who can't take a joke. Mostly that's true, but in their defense, look where they live: Russia. It's a bad neighborhood. To their north, nothing—south is to their north. To their south, China, over a billion *real* Communists ready to march four abreast over a cliff in a never-ending Malthusian parade. The Soviets are also on the same landmass with India.

"So what?" you say. "The Indians are peaceful. They don't even eat cows." But picture if you will what 750 million ravenous vegetarians could do to your potato patch.

It's an image that haunts the average Russian peasant. Recent research by Soviet psychiatrists has revealed the most common fear among their patients is a horde of starving Hindus pouring over the Himalayas like locusts, devouring everything green in sight.

The Soviets share a lengthy border with the lovely land of Iran, a mellow folk as we have seen. To the west they have their traditional allies—Polland, Hungary, Romania, friends you can count on. To the west of them, Germany. A nice neighbor historically. Sure, they get a little restless every thirty-five to forty years, but that's just a phase they go through.

Geography is only one of the Soviet millstones. The main problem is money, or rather rubles. There is a big difference between the two. Rubles aren't even considered money by most of the world. If you think it's hard to get rid of Canadian quarters, you ought to have a pocketful of kopeks.

The ruble has no exchange value in the international currency market. It's not even considered money in any country not occupied by Soviet troops. And even then it's only used to pay the soldiers. Rubles are not really money because they're only good in Russia and there's nothing to buy there. Rubles took a big dive on the world currency market when the bottom dropped out of the tundra-moss market. Russia's only valuable export anymore is cultural talent. Poets, ballet dancers, writers, anybody with feet. And in return, who defects to the Soviet Union? British homosexual spies, that's about it. We think we have a balance-of-trade problem. The collapse of communism was shockingly abrupt.

There was a demonstration in East Germany just after the wall fell that was so big France surrendered.

It was Robert Frost who said, "Something there is that doesn't love a wall." Now we know it's the East Germans. Three million of them crossed the first week the gates were opened. They came in droves to look at the stores to find out if all the stuff they saw on TV actually exists. These are people who were willing to risk death to escape to Poland a month earlier. To paraphrase Kennedy, there is no prouder boast for free people anywhere than "Ich bin ein Shopper."

What kicked off all these massive changes in the Communist world was the Soviet policy known as *glasnost*, which translates loosely as "Welcome back, sorry about the frostbite." Of course, the Russians have had periods of openness before: détente and de-Stalinization, to name two, but they turned out to be nothing more than new and improved variations on the old Russian political tactic known as "taking names." The KGB loosened up just long enough to see if anyone was really stupid enough to take advantage of it; then they started recruiting for the salt mines.

But this time I have hope. Gorbachev really seems like an old-fashioned liberal, even though the likelihood of a liberal rising to power in the Politburo is about the same as Jesse Jackson being elected governor of Utah. Sill, you never know. The Knicks might make the playoffs. For a Soviet premier, Gorbachev seems like a nice guy, and he's definitely not the most repressive leader in the world. He even got a Nobel Prize. On the other hand, so did Henry Kissinger.

To be fair, human rights are a fairly new concept to the Russian people. They're still getting used to the idea that power can change hands without twenty million people dying. What Gorbachev understands is that economic progress and human rights are inseparable. The reason America has such prosperity is that we have liberty and freedom. At least that's the conventional wisdom. The way I see it, the main difference between the Communists and the capitalists right now is that we can borrow money from the Japanese and they can't.

So before we start gloating about the demise of Communism and how superior we are, remember: if money is going to be the ultimate arbiter of the validity of a political philosophy, it's only a matter of time before we're kowtowing over coffee and doing calisthenics *en masse* at the factory every morning.

PART FIVE

The American Dream

WE LIVE in the catbird seat of the world. America, the beautiful; where else could a man step off the boat with nothing to his name but a loincloth and a pair of leg chains and spend his whole life singing in the fields? Where else could a man build his own railroad with nothing but a few carloads of rice, a couple of thousand coolies, and a land grant?

The eagle is the symbol of our nation, the very heart of my quest. To us it represents dignity, pride, and power.

The Indians had a different myth about the eagle. To them he was an arrogant bird who lorded it over earthbound man like some kind of high and mighty poobah, eating stinking fish and dropping excrement all over everyone, while the people on the ground shook their fists and fired off arrows that always fell short.

Then one day he was raining guano onto a tepee, laughing and carrying on, shaking his tail in mockery, and one of his feathers fell out. The man picked up the feather and fletched his arrow with it. With the eagle's own feather to guide it, the arrow flew straight and true and right to his heart. After that the tepees were a lot cleaner.

So to the Indians the eagle was the symbol of insufferable arrogance that eventually was destroyed by its stupidity. This is, of course, completely different from the way we look at our government today.

Perhaps a clue to what America is can be found in our symbols. The eagle on the great seal: He has an olive branch with thirteen leaves in one claw and thirteen arrows in the other. Everything is symbolic. His head is always turned toward the olive branch, which represents peace. The thirteen leaves represent the colonies, and the arrows represent the things he stole from the Indians.

The eagle has thirteen stars above his head and thirteen stripes on his chest. He has thirteen letters in his mouth that spell "E pluribus unum"—"one out of many." Everything is thirteen, so obviously he isn't planning to rely on good luck for anything.

Our national motto is "Novus ordo seclorum." It means "A new cycle of the ages." It's a very ambitious motto, but we've lived up to it.

Three thousand years ago Solomon said, "There is nothing new under the sun."

Later, Harry S Truman said, "The only thing new in the world is the history you don't know."

This only goes to show that there wasn't much history for people not to know back in Solomon's time. We've made a lot of it since then.

We certainly have had a fine place to make history: America, with an ocean view on either side. Canada to the north in case we ever run out of natural resources and Mexico to the south in case we ever need someone to work for minimum wage.

We have the Great Plains, with topsoil so rich it grows Asian people six feet tall in a single generation. We have mountain ranges made out of iron and coal, and the Great Northwest, where picnic tables and redwood fences grow on trees 300 feet tall. We have California, a place so mellow that the trees live to be 4,000 years old: the bristle-cone pines, the oldest living things on all the earth, and some of the ugliest and most useless. Which is why they got so old, I suppose.

But most of all, America is the land of opportunity, where you can get thirteen albums for a dollar ninety-nine. And if you have any ambition at all, you can change your address (and get thirteen more).

We've changed the world because we have something on our side more powerful than any dictator's army—greed. Every petty tyrant with a VCR and a bootleg "Dynasty" rerun can see for himself that it's more fun to live in a free country. What does it avail a man to rule his people with an iron fist if he can't get cable in his building?

Just to give one example. Thousands of Chinese exchange students came to America, and they did something unheard of in our educational system: They learned some of our history. They took it back to China and introduced the concept of individual liberty. Our Declaration of Independence says something that wakes people up: "That, to secure these rights (Life, Liberty, and so on), governments are instituted among men."

This is something Communists never

knew. They've been taught that governments are instituted to give party members a place to find jobs for their shiftless relatives.

In China they have no history of individual freedom or, for that matter, individual importance. The issue just doesn't even come up for discussion. Picture yourself an average Chinese—you're born, you're short, you have straight black hair. Why rock the boat?

There are a billion people in China. It's not easy to be an individual in a crowd of more than a billion people. Think of it. More than a *billion* people. That means even if you're a one-in-a-million type of guy, there are still a thousand guys exactly like you.

The first flickering lights of liberty were brutally crushed in Tiananmen Square, but heroes were made that will never be forgotten as long as free men keep history.

We know that many escaped the manhunt following Tiananmen Square to spread the gospel of freedom. Perhaps they were somehow able to lose themselves in the crowd. It can't be that hard in China. One of the world's most difficult jobs has to be police sketch artist in Beijing.

China may seem asleep for the moment, but like all the world, it soon will be dreaming the American Dream.

It's a dream that takes many forms. JFK dreamed that men would go to the moon and plant the flag of peace for all mankind. And LBJ made it come true, on some property a few friends of his owned in Houston. Ronald Reagan also had a dream about space, something about an umbrella, with lasers, and X rays, but he was never really awake long enough to think it through.

One of the greatest of American dreamers was Martin Luther King. His dream was that "my four little children will one day live in a nation where they are not judged by the color of their skin, but by the content of their character."

It was an American Dream, and it inspired the world. Even I have a dream. In my dream, I go to a job interview, but I'm not wearing any pants. Obviously, you can't base a national policy on it.

But it does go to show that not all men are created equal. Some men have greater dreams than others. Americans have always had big dreams. What makes us Americans is that the few among us with great dreams have the freedom to make them come true. It's something worth believing in.

And that's The Big Picture.

Index

INDEX

Bork, Robert, 53
Born agains, 85, 88
Boston Harbor, 121
Brawley, Tawana, 145
Breach-of-contract birth, 89
British define themselves, 13
Brown, A. Whitney
  childhood and adolescence of, 34–47
  Indian blood of, 137–138
  and sanctity of life, 85–88
Buddha, 43, 44
Bundy, Ted, 54
Bush, George
  and contras, 55
  as Education President, 73, 92–93
  as Environmental President, 73, 121
  inauguration of, 75–77
  new world order of, 155–156
  and Persian Gulf war, 155–156
  personal touch of, 73, 75, 82
  as politician, 64, 77, 82, 121
  presidency of, 73–82

California initiative process, 104
Canada and Canadians, 14, 31, 69, 169
Cancer, 7
  chemical-induced, 127–128
Cannon fodder, education of, 96
Capital gains, 81, 97
Capitalists, Communists vs., 164
Carnegie, Andrew, 15
Carter, Jimmy, 56, 57, 62
Castro, Fidel, 74
Catastrophic Health Plan, 51
Catholics, 81, 109
Censorship, 5–6
Chain letter, the deficit and, 115
Champollion, J.-J., 7
Charlemagne, 29
Chernobyl, 131–133
Cherokees, 140–141
Childhood, American, 83–84
China and Chinese, 38, 160, 167
  and American dream, 171
  curses, 11
  exchange students, 170–171
  Great Wall, 18
  Tiananmen Square, 171

Christ, 44
Christian fundamentalists, 5, 64, 85, 88, 122
Christmas tree, vegetarian assaults, 124–125
Chrysler, 114
CIA front companies, 108
Civil Rights Act, 42, 102
Civil rights movement, 39–40, 42
Civil War (U.S.), 69, 151
CNN, 11, 154
Cocaine, economics of, 51, 56, 93, 106, 109
Cold war, 12
Collins, Michael, 23
Colombia, 110
Columbia Pictures, 59
Columbus, Christopher, 140, 150
Commercials, TV, 9–10
Communism, 12
  capitalism vs., 164
  collapse of, 12, 33, 57, 157, 159–164
  threat to Latin America, 150–151
Condos, 107
Congress, 99–104
  corruption of, 100–102
  election of, 102–104
  quality of, 100–101
  salary increase for, 99–102
  whining constituents and, 103
Connally, John, 40
Constituents, whining, 103
Constitutional amendments, flag burning and, 77–81
Constitution (U.S.), 30
Consumerism
  and debt, 53
  TV and, 10
Contras, 55, 93, 94, 108, 109, 150–151
Corruption, political. See Congress
Cosby, Bill, 145
Crack, 9, 51, 77, 83, 94, 97, 147, 160
Crack babies, 83–84
Crap, etymology of, 24
Crapper, Thomas, 24
Cronkite, Walter, 38
C-SPAN, 9, 101
Culture, American, 7. See also Con-

INDEX

Culture, American (*cont.*)
sumerism; Drugs; Illiteracy;
Racism
Cuomo, Mario, 83
Current events, 11, 15
Custer, George A., 17, 139

Daley, Richard, 41
Dead (band), 42
Debt and deficit, American, 52–53,
105–115
Decade of the Child, 83, 88
Declaration of Independence, 31–
34, 103, 170
Defense Department, 128
Democrats, 80
Southern, 41
Desert, 20–21
Détente, 163
Detroit, racism in, 144
Diamond, Neil, 22
Discrimination, 148. *See also* Racism
Dole, Bob, 64
Dole, Elizabeth, 82
Drugs, 9, 40, 43, 51, 54, 56, 77, 83–
84, 93, 97, 106
"just say no," 57, 110
trade deficit and, 112
war on, 57, 74, 93–94, 154
Dukakis, Kitty, 66
Dukakis, Michael, 66, 76
Dumping, by and on Japanese,
112–113

Eagle, as American symbol, 167–
168
Earth Day, New York, 125
Eastern Europe, 33, 58, 157, 161
as market, 114
Ecological disasters
Chernobyl, 131–133
Earth Day, New York, 125
Exxon Valdez, 119–122, 125
Ecology, 20
Economic management, 110
Education
American, 84, 91–98. *See also*
Illiteracy
of cannon fodder, 96
in New York, 92, 96
Education President, 73, 92–93

Egypt, 62
and Persian Gulf war, 155
pyramids, 7, 18, 21
Eighties, 49–60, 73, 80
Eisenhower, Dwight, 38
Elderly, commercials for, 10
Electoral process, 61–71, 102–104
El Salvador, 151
Environment, 119–126. *See also*
Ecological disasters
Environmental President, 73, 121
Equality, 33–34
EST, 44
Eurasians, 146
Evolution, 87–88
Extinction of species, 11, 122–123,
125
Exxon spokesmen, 120–121
Exxon Valdez, 119–122, 125

Farm crisis, pot and, 111
Farmers as electorate, 68
FICA tax, 107
Fifties, 35, 37–39
First Amendment, 30, 77
First Commandment, 80. *See also*
Flag burning
Flag burning, 77–81
Ford, 113
Founding Fathers, 31, 33
France and French
arm Iraq, 152–153
define themselves, 14
hygiene of, 13, 138
Indians and, 138
nuclear tests, 130–131
and Persian Gulf war, 155
Franklin, Benjamin, 32
Frost, Robert, 162
Fujisankei hires ex-President,
59
Fundamentalists, 5, 64, 122

General Dynamics, 128–129
Generational gap, economics of,
97–98
Genghis Khan, 29
Geography, 150
Russian, 160–161
George III, King, 103
Gephardt, Richard, 64–65, 112
no eyebrows handicap, 65

INDEX

INDEX

INDEX

INDEX

INDEX